A War of Frontier and Empire

A WAR *of* FRONTIER *and* EMPIRE

THE PHILIPPINE-AMERICAN WAR, 1899–1902

DAVID J. SILBEY

HILL AND WANG

A DIVISION OF FARRAR, STRAUS AND GIROUX

NEW YORK

Hill and Wang
A division of Farrar, Straus and Giroux
18 West 18th Street, New York 10011

Copyright © 2007 by David J. Silbey
All rights reserved
Distributed in Canada by D&M Publishers, Inc.
Printed in the United States of America
Published in 2007 by Hill and Wang
First paperback edition, 2008

The Library of Congress has cataloged the hardcover edition as follows:
Silbey, David.
A war of frontier and empire : the Philippine-American war, 1899–1902 /
David J. Silbey.— 1st ed.
   p.   cm.
Includes bibliographical references (p.   ) and index.
ISBN-13: 978-0-8090-7187-6 (hardcover : alk. paper)
ISBN-10: 0-8090-7187-8 (hardcover : alk. paper)
   1. Philippines—History—Philippine American War, 1899–1902.
I. Title.

DS679 .S57 2007
959.9'031—dc22

2006009305

Paperback ISBN-13: 978-0-8090-9661-9
Paperback ISBN-10: 0-8090-9661-7

Designed by Debbie Glasserman

www.fsgbooks.com

3   5   7   9   10   8   6   4   2

For Mari

A Note on Names

To remain true to the sources, place names have been used as found, without an attempt to modernize.

Contents

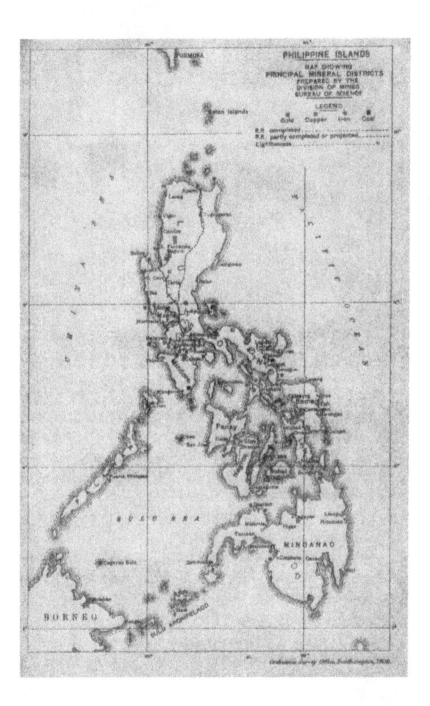

PHILIPPINE ISLANDS

MAP SHOWING
PRINCIPAL MINERAL DISTRICTS
PREPARED BY THE
DIVISION OF MINES
BUREAU OF SCIENCE

LEGEND
Gold   Copper   Iron   Coal

R.R. completed.........................
R.R. partly completed or projected.........
Lighthouse............................

Introduction:
The Urgency of the Asking

For Americans, it was a war of frontier, and of empire. It was a war that brought together the dominant American experience of the nineteenth century, the chaotic and defining expansion westward, with a new and at times uncomfortable imperial ambition. Manifest destiny, though still powerful, seemed less manifest and more ambiguous; less fate than one path among many. Americans had come to feel that the continent was perhaps too small to contain them and their nation. But what form was American entry into global power to take? The war did not provide an answer, but it did confirm the urgency of the asking.

That energetic American nationalism would have been unfamiliar to most Filipinos. In fact, to label the inhabitants of the Philippines as Filipinos in 1899 would be to use a misnomer. Few Filipinos felt an overarching sense of the archipelago as a single united nation. Ordinary loyalties to region, to patron, or to family were much more likely. The war they fought was, in many ways, a war of those loyalties. Thus, while the Western powers fighting for dominance in the Philippine Archipelago—Spain and the United States—were relatively unitary actors, the forces resisting them were not. There was, despite the later assumption of both Filipino historians and post–Vietnam War American historians, no Philippine nation. There was no single central conception of state and nation that animated those fighting (or not fighting) against their colonial powers. There was, instead, a shaky coalition of groups that resisted. These groups were fundamentally different in their strategies and tactics, and the attention they paid to the titular leader of the revolution, Emilio Aguinaldo, varied greatly, even before his capture in 1901. They were made up of different ethnic groups, speaking different languages, and fighting in different ways.

But a peculiar thing happened. The Philippine-American War became, as seen dimly in retrospect, a war of national striving. At the time it was not a revolutionary war, in the same pungent and independent sense that Americans think of their revolution. But in the decades afterward the war became that kind of conflict, held up as the first unified Filipino experience of the modern era. Many had fought and almost everyone had experienced the war. Because of that, it gained status as a first struggle for independence and national pride. "To understand the Filipino-American War," a Philippine historian said, "is to understand a large part of the groundwork of contemporary Philippine society."[1]

This retroactive reordering sometimes has odd effects.

For example, what should we call the conflict? War? Revolution? Insurgency? All of those labels have been applied, and all have been disputed. Who was the United States fighting? The Philippines? Filipinos? A Tagalog insurgency? These too have all been suggested and criticized.

Could the conflict even be called a war? By the standards of the day, sovereignty had passed legitimately from the Spanish to the Americans, the Philippines had not been an independent nation for centuries before that, and the inhabitants of the Philippines did not conceive of themselves as part of a single unified social, political, and cultural body. If there was no Philippine nation to engage in war or be conquered, then would not labeling the fight a "war" be a grave misrepresentation? In such an analysis what happened in the archipelago from 1899 to 1902 was an insurgency, not a war.

Filipino historians starting in the 1950s saw the conflict as one of a nascent nation coming into its own, cruelly subjugated first by the Spanish and then by the United States. They explicitly denied such an interpretation. This Filipino nation had become unified under the lash of war, and had fought—if unsuccessfully—against its conquerors. The war was a war. To reduce it to an "insurgency," these historians believed, was to betray that nation, and was to take part in a larger effort to subjugate the Filipinos and their past. Filipino history, Renato Constantino wrote, had been "used to capture [Filipino] minds" and make them believe that their "conquerors" were really "altruistic and self-abnegating partners."[2]

How, then, should we refer to it? There are arguments of merit on both sides of the question, and—as frustratingly usual in history—arriving at a definitive conclusion is diffi-

cult. Brian Linn, for one, simply avoids the issue by refer-
ring to the conflict as the "War in the Philippines."[3] But
perhaps we can place a layer of sophistication over the issue.
At the time of the conflict, the Philippine nation was barely
formed. Tagalogs, Moros, and the other Filipino tribal
groups did not connect themselves to each other in a single, imagined community. Local loyalties—whether tribal
or client/patron—remained more powerful than national
ones. This certainly changed during the war, and, at its
height, it could be argued than the Philippines was closer to
sociocultural unity than at any time before. But the islands
ruled by the United States after 1902 were still only a single
unit in an administrative sense. Having said that, however,
the legal argument that sovereignty passed without inter-
ruption from the Spanish to the Americans should be
treated with some skepticism. By the standards of the day,
the handover from Spain to the United States was indeed
transacted according to law and custom. But any number
of treaties during this period—the 1885 Treaty of Berlin to
name but one example—legally handed over the rule of captive peoples to one Western power or another. That such
handovers gave anyone, American or otherwise, anything
but the most formal sort of "sovereignty" is open to question. Moral suasion did not come hand in hand with dominance.

While the conflict at the time was hardly a war between
two sovereign nations, for Filipinos, that struggle became
the central event of their national myth. They reimposed
the idea of a nation onto the warring tribes of 1899–1902,
and traced the birth of the idea of a larger Filipino nation to
those years. Though there was no Filipino nation in the
conflict, the Filipino nation could not have existed without

the war. To label it an insurgency ignores that foundational importance.

Finally, there is the quiet misgiving that comes from refusing to call a conflict what the people most intimately affected by it would prefer. Too much of Philippine history has been organized and conceptually framed from an outsider's perspective. A series of imperial masters—Spanish, American, and Japanese—have ruled the Philippines and ruled histories of the archipelago. Even the names of the historical eras—"Later Spanish Colonialism," "American Colonialism," "the Japanese Occupation"—reflect this.[4] When it comes down to it, the conflict was fought in the islands, Filipinos fought and died (on both sides) in it, and they may well have earned the right to call it what they wish. Unless we are willing to call the North American period from 1776 to 1783 the Colonial Insurgency, perhaps we should honor that wish. Thus, while understanding all the caveats, complaints, hedges, and ambiguities connected with it, I shall nonetheless refer to the conflict of 1899–1902 as the Philippine-American War.

Before leaving off this discussion, let me point out one more thing. Whether we refer to 1899–1902 as an insurgency, a revolution, or a war, we are essentially implying that it was a single event or collection of events. That, as we shall see, is not true. If anything, the war is better understood as three separate and distinct conflicts. The first was a war between the Spanish and the allied United States and Filipino forces. The second was a conventional war between the U.S. Army and Navy and the Army of Liberation of the Philippine Republic. The third was a guerrilla war between the U.S. Army and Navy and an insurgent alliance of remnants of the Army of Liberation and other groups. The three conflicts happened consecutively but differed significantly. Lumping them together under one name dangerously obscures those differences, something we should bear in mind as we go. A name, however carefully considered, is not the thing itself. As always with historical events, the name is merely shorthand for the multitude, for the people, places, and events sprawling untidily through the chronology. That multitude is the subject of this book.

A War of Frontier and Empire

One

A WAR OF FRONTIER AND EMPIRE

A Summit

President Emilio Aguinaldo sat beneath a mountain one December day of 1899 and wondered what had happened to his revolution. More than a year before, he had been the head of an Army of Liberation which controlled the great majority of the Philippine Islands. The Filipinos of that army had swept aside their centuries-long imperial over-lord, the Spanish. All that remained for them was to take the capital city of Manila and declare themselves an independent republic.

Manila did fall, but not to the Filipinos. Instead, a force of Americans won a series of shattering naval and military battles, captured Manila from under the noses of the revolutionary army, and then had the temerity to *buy* the islands from the Spanish crown. What the Filipinos had paid for in blood, the Americans had paid for with gold.

Aguinaldo found to his sorrow that he could do little to prevent it. The follow-on conflict between the Americans and the Filipinos had run almost entirely the Americans' way. Filipino defeat had been so stunning and complete that Aguinaldo had been forced to dissolve his government and army in mid-November 1899 and flee into hiding, hoping to reconstitute his forces as a guerrilla army and shadow republic.

He could not even guarantee his own safety. Fleeing the central plains of Luzon in mid-November 1899, Aguinaldo was pursued by relentless American forces who were not stopped even by the near-total sacrifice of a Filipino rearguard. His bolthole, in the northern valleys, had been surrendered by a treacherous general. So now Aguinaldo, in mid-December, sat in the small settlement of Banane on the slope of Mount Polis and wondered what he should do. He could not stay there. The Americans were likely to catch up soon; in any case, Banane was inhabited by the Igorots, tribal warriors of uncertain loyalties. Aguinaldo and his escort had been greeted when they arrived by the *kanao*, an Igorot ceremony celebrating the taking of a trophy: the head, hands, and feet of an enemy. Whether the Igorots intended this as a warning is not clear, but Aguinaldo certainly took it as one. He and his sister, one of a number of women accompanying the group, wistfully discussed traveling in Europe once the war was over. Such fantasies, however, did nothing for the short term.

Thus, on the night of December 16, in a grove near his camp, Aguinaldo called a council of war. He and his officers and political associates discussed what to do. The discussion was reluctant and difficult, with several officers refusing to give their opinion and preferring simply to follow Aguinaldo's lead. Aguinaldo himself remained cagey. Finally, Simeon Villa, one of his medical officers, spoke up and suggested that the group "should separate from the women, who constitute such a great impediment or obstacle to any plan," and continue deeper into the mountainous highlands to find a place to hide and continue the fight. To this Aguinaldo agreed, and so committed himself to going on with the war, hoping that conventional defeat might be followed by irregular victory. He left behind family, friends, and allies to wage this guerrilla war, one that would last a further two years. That decision would not bring the Filipinos victory, but Aguinaldo would live to see the day that independence came to the islands, and know that it had in some small way originated in the efforts of the 1890s.[1]

Geography and Colonization

The geography of the Philippines imposes a sense of disconnectedness. Thousands of islands, roughly sprinkled through the western Pacific, make up the archipelago. The distances between the islands vary from a few hundred yards to many miles. It is possible to swim easily from Leyte to Samar, while Palawan sits by itself to the west, stretching for hundreds of miles into the Sulu Sea. At their farthest south the Philippines reach within a few dozen miles of the island of Borneo. At their northernmost limit the islands come close to Taiwan. To the west is the South China Sea, surrounded in the late nineteenth century by the colonial outposts of a range of European powers: French Indochina due west, British Hong Kong northwest, and the Dutch East Indies southwest. And looming over all was the massive, ponderous, and decayed Chinese empire, home to hundreds of millions and bloated by centuries of lacquered ritual. By the turn of the century China was less a nation than a prize: a target that every major power eyed with anticipation.

To the east was the Philippine Sea, an open swath of ocean bounded by New Guinea on the south, a necklace of small islands farther east, and, to the north, Japan. By the last few decades of the nineteenth century, the power of newly industrialized Japan was becoming apparent. The Japanese had not yet had their coming-out party, the moment they stepped onto the world stage and announced themselves as a power of substance. That would come a few years later in the Russo-Japanese War of 1904–1905.

In the middle of all this was the sleepy Spanish colony of the Philippines. Imperial Spain had acquired the islands centuries before, during the burst of exploration that marked the fifteenth and sixteenth centuries. Magellan had planted the Spanish flag there in 1521, and had planted himself as well, after an ill-considered meeting with hostile natives. Only one of Magellan's ships returned, captained by his first mate, Juan Sebastián de Elcano, who made it home, but, somewhat unfairly, not into historical memory. The Spanish were not the first outsiders to visit the Philippines. Certainly the great Chinese fleets of the late fifteenth and early sixteenth centuries had stopped by. And Muslim explorers had broken out of the Indian Ocean even earlier, settling in some of the southern islands. But only the Spanish came to stay throughout the archipelago. In the 1560s, led by Don Miguel López de Legazpi, who became the first governor and captain-general of the islands, they arrived in force, aggressive, imperialistic, and awash in the gold and silver of Central America. Spanish overlordship of the Philippines was more benign than their control of Central America. Critically, without silver and gold to mine, the Spanish had less need of slave labor to work to death in the dark underground. Instead, the Philippines, and the city of Manila in particular, served as the primary trading hub for the Spanish in the Pacific. They shipped silver from Mexico to Manila every year—the Pacific counterpart to the famous Atlantic flota that so obsessed pirates and privateers like Sir Francis Drake in the sixteenth century. From China came junks carrying silk and other precious items. The two met in Manila, and there the goods were exchanged for the enrichment of both sides.

The Spanish brought with them a well-established body of law to organize and run the colonies, developed in the hard laboratory of Central America. Governors-general of the islands were, for the first few centuries, experienced men from either the Americas or from Spanish Flanders. The result was a thriving and sophisticated economy in the Philippines, a fierce trade rivalry with Portuguese merchants based at the Chinese port of Macao, and, not least, a growing Chinese population in the Philippines.[2] It would not be the last time that the importance of the Philippines was seen largely for its relationship with China.

The Spanish also brought with them a structured set of economic relationships, based on the domination of a Spanish elite, and a series of client-patron relations that would characterize the Philippines for centuries to come. People defined themselves in a complicated web of social networks in which a relatively small number of wealthy

Spanish held the allegiance of hundreds if not thousands of both Spaniards and Filipinos. To call these relationships landlord-tenant would be to oversimplify desperately. The client-patron relationship might include landlordism and tenantship, but it was rarely limited to mere geographical allegiance. Clients looked to their patrons for a whole range of economic, social, and cultural protections, and patrons looked to their clients for corresponding services.

Catholicism and Empire

But perhaps the most critical European import was Catholicism, and all the trappings of that church: priests, the Latin Mass, and the Inquisition. The lack of Spanish government interest in anything outside of Manila left the field open for the clergy, and the Catholic church—fired with the energies of the Counter-Reformation—soon developed an extensive network throughout the Philippines that, unlike almost anywhere else in Asia, converted a substantial majority of the populace to Catholicism. Many Filipinos might see no Spaniard but a friar for their entire lives. The conversions were long-lasting but not universal. Though the populations of the northern islands largely became Catholic, many in the southern islands remained true to their first conversion, to Islam.

This reliance on the church for governing most of the Philippines had, however, an interesting side effect. Conversion was accomplished in the native dialects while masses were in Latin. The result was that, throughout Spanish control of the islands, the great majority of Filipinos never learned the tongue of the imperial motherland. A universal language was never imposed on the colony. The archipelago instead remained something of a Tower of Babel, with hundreds of groups speaking different dialects and unable, to a large extent, to understand one another.[3]

Spanish power reached its height in the last half of the sixteenth century under King Philip II. But imperial Spain was—as happened so often with great powers—economically overstretched by its wars, its empire, and its appetites. Despite the massive influx of monies from the Central American mines, the Spanish throne went bankrupt a number of times during the sixteenth and seventeenth centuries. The eighty-year revolution in the Spanish Netherlands, the Thirty Years' War of 1618–48, and the rise of Dutch, English, and, especially, French power doomed Spain to a long, slow slide from the top ranks.

Her empire decayed along with her. The Thirty Years' War, fought on a global scale against the Dutch, proved especially difficult for Spanish colonies.[4] The Philippines themselves were taken briefly by the British in the middle of the eighteenth century, only to be handed back in a peace treaty, largely because the British were not interested in keeping them. The Central and South American colonies broke away in the first decades of the nineteenth century in a series of revolts that Spain could not prevent or defeat. Spanish Florida fell to the United States shortly thereafter. What was left of the empire by the late nineteenth century were remnants: islands scattered through the Caribbean, headlined by Cuba and Puerto Rico, and in the Pacific, the Philippines. Spain held them not by power but by indifference. None of the other great powers could be bothered to take them.

Nor had the nineteenth century been kind to the Philippines. The Industrial Revolution sweeping through the Western nations had made the Philippines into part of the global hinterland that fed raw materials into the voracious factories of Europe. Unlike the previous few centuries, when the Philippines were largely shut off from the world economy, the demands of the Industrial Revolution levered the Philippine economy open. From the Philippines came the raw agricultural product needed by the factories and back to the Philippines went the manufactures of those factories. Manila, Iloilo, and Cebu became, by the end of the century, large trading ports through which most of the Philippine economic transactions took place.[5]

The result was demographic upheaval, as populations shifted in adjustment to the new economy. Hundreds of thousands moved inland—most particularly into the great central plains of Luzon—to clear the land and turn it over to the production of agricultural goods like tobacco and abaca fiber, which could then be sold to industrial nations. This frontier, inland rather than westward, created a society that—oddly—resembled nothing so much as the American West. "The Philippines had pioneers and wagon trains, cattle ranching and rustling, cowboys and bandits, railroad building. . . ."[6]

But the breakdown of traditional societal arrangements resulted in an increased number of mortality crises throughout the Philippines, in which death rates spiked because of disease, famine, and dislocation. The 1880s were a "decade of death" for the Philippines,[7] and the 1890s were not much better. The province of the Batangas on the island of Luzon experienced a smallpox epidemic in 1889 and a cholera epidemic in 1890, and lost most of its coffee crops to disease in the first years of the 1890s. In addition, the cattle disease rinderpest killed thousands of water buffalo, the main domestic farm animal of the Philippines.[8]

The result was a society in economic and social flux in the 1880s and 1890s. The Spanish government contributed to this social instability by first appointing a series of reforming governors from 1880 to 1888 who opened up Philippine society and allowed limited political and cultural freedom, and then appointing the reactionary Gen. Valeriano Weyler to the governorship from 1888 to 1891, who undid the reforms, embittering many Filipinos.[9]

Revolution

This was the situation when the last decade of the nineteenth century opened. A declining Spanish monarchy, its gaze turned inward to past glories, ruled over a Philippines riven by demographic and economic difficulties. It should not come as a surprise that something approaching a revolution began. What started was less an organized attempt to throw off Spanish rule than an effort of different groups to shape violently the unsteady social order around them.

To understand the revolution, we must understand the racial divisions within Philippine society. At the top were the *peninsulares*, Spaniards born in Spain. Below them were *insulares* (also simply called Filipinos), Spaniards born in the Philippines. Below them, far below them, were the *indios*, non-Spanish native-born Filipinos. The Spanish—peninsulare and insulare—dominated the Philippine society and economy. The indios—even the term had racist connotations—were forever ruled rather than rulers: "The monkey will always be a monkey however you dress him with shirt and trousers," was one friar's summation in 1885.[10]

But things began to shift slightly in the last part of the nineteenth century. Upper-class Filipinos began to send their children abroad to be educated in Europe. This group came to be known as *ilustrados*. Among them was a young Filipino named José Rizal. In 1889 Rizal and his friends were touring Europe where they went to see the Paris Exposition of that year. At the Exposition they saw a Wild West show, which included Native American performers on horseback. Struck by the daring and popularity of the performers, Rizal and his friends decided to form an association for Filipinos to assert their own identity, to make themselves "braves" on the American Indian model. Los Indios Bravos, they called it, a spectacular entangling of Spanish and American themes and ideas.

Rizal positioned his group not as one grasping to elevate itself to the level of the Spanish-born elite, but as one seeking common cause with the indio. The group explicitly denied the power and righteousness of Spanish and Catholic control of the islands by basing its appeal to power in the native population. At the same time, his appropriation of an American frontier motif connected Los Indios Bravos to that more open social mythos. The Filipinos would be warrior Indians resisting the imperial domination of their civilized overlords. Rizal had already appropriated another American theme in an 1887 protest novel whose title echoed one of the slogans of the American Revolution: *Noli me tangere* (Touch Me Not).[11] The irony of such appeals to American models was only equalled a half century later, when Ho Chi Minh stole chunks of the Declaration of Independence to declare Vietnamese autonomy in 1945.

If this revolution—or revolutions—sounds chaotic, it was. What broke out in the mid-1890s consisted of various groups led by leaders with various motives who shared a distaste for Spanish control but felt something less than love for one another. Perhaps none of the divisions was more critical than the ethnic one. The Tagalogs—who dominated the revolution throughout this period—were held in suspicion by other Filipinos.[12] But the Filipinos were divided on economic grounds as well. Wealthy Philippine landowners wished for freedom from the Spanish but did not seek to restructure the economy or the society of the Philippines. Theirs was a conservative vision of revolution, one that would send the Spanish home and leave the landowners still in charge. Their eventual champion was Emilio Aguinaldo y Famy, of mixed Chinese and Tagalog ancestry, whose father was a small-time politician in Cavite.[13]

Other groups were more mixed economically and ethnically. One of the larger of these groups was the Katipunan, led by a revolutionary named Andres Bonifacio. Members of the Katipunan came from different economic and social groups within Philippine society, for the most part from the tenant farmers of the countryside and the middle classes of the cities. Like many others, the Katipunan were poorly equipped, poorly organized, poorly led, and prone to divisiveness. They squabbled with other groups and amongst themselves. That much later Bonifacio would become seen as a national hero had less to do with his own actions than with the need in a newly independent country for something akin to founding fathers.

Bonifacio and Aguinaldo soon clashed. Bonifacio believed fervently in his cause, but he was naive in his dealings both with the Spanish and with Aguinaldo. Aguinaldo, whatever his other faults, proved something of an adept politician. He soon outmaneuvered Bonifacio, getting himself elected president of the revolutionary government in early 1897. Not satisfied with that, he had Bonifacio arrested and tried on trumped-up charges of treason and executed on May 10, 1897. Aguinaldo later claimed that he had commuted the sentence, but that by the sheerest bad luck the commutation did not arrive in time to prevent Bonifacio's execution. From then until his capture in 1901, Aguinaldo would be the closest thing that the Philippines had to a native national leader.

His leadership was never going to produce radical change. It might evict the Spanish, but it would never remake Philippine society. Though Renato Constantino is perhaps exaggerating when he says that Aguinaldo "led the force that preempted the revolution," the government and society that resulted from a victorious insurgency by the Aguinaldo-led Filipinos would likely have strongly resembled a pre-insurgency Philippines in structure and control.[14]

The chaos of the revolution was lucky for the enfeebled Spanish, for perhaps the only enemy they could have defeated was this one, forever teetering on the edge of dissolution. The Spanish army won most of the battles of 1897, driving revolutionary forces out of strongholds in places like Cavite and Talisay in the Batangas. In response, Aguinaldo signaled to the Spanish that he was open to negotiation. In July 1897, a revolutionary manifesto was published under the nom de plume of "Malabar." In form it was similar to an earlier one put out by Aguinaldo, making it clear that he was the author. It laid out a series of demands on the Spanish, including a parliament for the Philippines, freedom of the press, and religious freedom. But it conceded, implicitly, continued Spanish sovereignty over the islands.

The signal was received. In August 1897 the Spanish governor, Primo de Rivera, issued an amnesty for those who would turn themselves in, and sent a native lawyer, Pedro Paterno, to negotiate with Aguinaldo. Paterno carried no more than vague promises and statements that he had overheard the governor speak of reform, but Aguinaldo greeted him happily, releasing a number of Spanish prisoners as a show of good faith. The negotiations, which took place in the rebel town of Biak-na-Bato, resulted in the Treaty of Biak-na-Bato, signed on December 14, 1897.

It is hard to see the treaty as anything but a victory for the Spanish. Though early drafts put forward by Aguinaldo had contained some demands for reform, the final copy of the treaty in essence traded the end of the rebellion by the Filipinos in return for large sums paid to Aguinaldo and his closest advisers, and their removal to Hong Kong. Whether the removal should be referred to as "exile," as Aguinaldo would have liked, or "protective custody," as perhaps his fellow Filipinos would have preferred, was open to debate. Primo de Rivera remarked that "chief among the wishes" of Aguinaldo was that his "future be assured" and that he (and his associates) be given "indispensable means of subsistence."[15] The "means" in this case consisted of 800,000 Spanish pesetas, quite enough to set Aguinaldo up comfortably in Hong Kong.

The terms of the treaty were only loosely lived up to, by both sides. In the end Aguinaldo and the leadership found themselves in Hong Kong with 400,000 pesetas of Spanish money, half of Spain's commitment. To his credit, Aguinaldo deposited most of the money in a bank for future use in service of the revolution. He kept enough to live comfortably, and there are indications that some of the other leaders were not particularly pleased with this virtuous disposition of the cash.[16]

That was the situation as the year turned from 1897 to 1898. How much of the Philippines the Spanish actually controlled is not clear. They certainly ruled the major cities and essentially controlled the economic infrastructure of the colony. Since the value of the Philippines as an imperial possession had always been in the trade that flowed through the major cities, whether silk from China or agricultural goods from the interior, that seemed enough to them.

America Enters, Stage Right

But here another actor entered the scene, late-arriving but still crucial. The United States of America was, in many ways, the complete antithesis of Spain. Where Spain dreamed somnolently of past glories, the United States looked forward to future achievements. Where Spain had a long and storied history that stretched back centuries, if not millennia, the United States looked back to its founding barely a century before. Where Spain's geography was littered with the leftovers of great empires that had surged and receded over her terrain—from the Roman arches of roads and aqueducts to the delicate minarets and graceful Moorish architecture of the Muslim emirates—the United States prided itself (truthfully or not) in having created itself in a virgin territory. Where Spain seemed simply to be fighting to preserve the remnants of empire, the United States be-

lieved that it had a manifest destiny to expand and dominate the American continent.

The second half of the nineteenth century for the United
States had been dominated by the most catastrophic war in
American history, the Civil War of 1861–65. That conflict,
a sectional struggle over the peculiar institution of slavery,
had killed more than 600,000 Americans, devastated large
areas of Pennsylvania, Virginia, Georgia, and the Carolinas,
and seen gallantry and horror in large measures. For a moment in 1865, the United States stood as one of the world's
great military powers, with an experienced army over a mil-
lion strong and a large and advanced navy. The victorious
Union could stand with any of the great nations of Europe,
a position confirmed when, in a quarrel with the French
over their Mexican puppet emperor, Maximilian, the threat
of American military power forced the emperor Napo-
leon III into a humiliating retreat.

But that military power evaporated almost immediately
after the end of the war. Both army and navy shrank dramatically. The ships were mothballed or scrapped. The soldiers were demobilized and sent home, their equipment
destroyed or stored. By 1875 the U.S. Army could muster
about 25,000 men. The French army was twenty times
larger, the British seven times, and even the Belgian army
was twice as large. This military served a nation that simply
was not interested in matters martial. It was a nation in
which upon being introduced to an army officer in 1885, a
woman could reply: "What, a colonel of the Army? Why, I
supposed the Army was all disbanded at the close of the
war!"[17]

For both enlisted men and officers, pay and conditions
in that "disbanded" army were execrable. The wage for sol-

diers was low and infrequently raised. Equipment was antiquated. Food and supplies were second-rate; pilfering was
common. Soldiers were usually stationed in isolated forts,
without recreation or distraction. The answer to most of
this was alcohol, and both officers and men imbibed large
quantities. In 1886, when George Duncan, who had just
graduated from West Point, reported for duty at Fort
Wingate, he found that the entire fort was in the middle of
a five-day drinking spree.[18]

Such neglect meant that men enlisted to serve only out
of desperation, whether by "absolute want," as Col. Richard
Dodge put it in 1885, or because they were recent immi-
grants and could find no other work. They were "a terribly
rough, tough lot," as George Marshall remembered them,
and they deserted frequently. From 1867 to 1891, one-
seventh of the army deserted every year.[19]

Career prospects for officers were terrible. They had
come into the army together during the Civil War. Because
of this, generals were frequently the same age or only a bit
older than those they ranked. In 1893 the average captain
was only four years younger than the average general. Without casualties, without expansion, and with few retire-
ments, officers were frequently stuck in their rank for
decades. Arthur MacArthur had been promoted to the rank
of lieutenant colonel during the Civil War. At the end, he
had reverted to first lieutenant. Promoted to captain shortly
thereafter, he remained a captain for twenty-three years,
and did not attain his old rank until the 1890s. One officer,
John Bigelow, said of the situation:

> What an inglorious way of advancing, that of merely re-
> placing those who topple over, and what an unfortunate

line of aspiration that leads to self-congratulations at the
death of a friend.[20]

Bigelow's point was well taken: promotions in the Seventh
Cavalry jumped after the slaughter of George Custer and
his command.

The army's situation began to change a bit in the early
1890s. As the frontier disappeared, posts in the West were
closed up and consolidated. There were 175 such forts in
1870. By 1894 there were only 80. In addition, under President Benjamin Harrison, a program of gradually modern-
izing army equipment and organization was begun, though
slowly and in fits and starts. Bringing in new blood could
hardly be avoided; the Civil War generation of soldiers
was beginning to age, and younger officers, like Archibald
Campbell in 1889, started making unkind remarks about
their superiors "tottering around in their dotage." Campbell
could be forgiven, as his commanding officer was a veteran
not only of the Civil War but of the Mexican War of
1846–48.[21] But the reform did not excite the imagination
of the nation. The only wars that the United States might
plausibly be expected to fight were in the western hemisphere, and its potential opponents there did not seem particularly threatening. Because of this, there was little push
to create a modern army from the civilian side. The single
exception to this, beginning in the 1890s, was a growing effort to modernize the coastal defense system with modern
fortifications and artillery.

There was, however, more of a push from within the
army itself. Led by, among others, Gen. William T. Sherman of Civil War fame, the army began to create a structure
for professionalization. This included the rationalization

and organization of officer training and the establishment of advanced schools for officers at places like Fort Leavenworth, Kansas. The effect was to create the structure and organization for a much larger and more professional army, if only the funding and will could be found to create one. The alterations were drastic enough that in 1890, the inspector general of the army could say that "one year enforces changes as great as a century once caused."[22] He was perhaps optimistic, but not delusional.

This emphasis on professionalization would continue throughout the 1890s, and be accelerated by the difficulties of the Spanish-American War and the Philippine War. The flaws found therein would lead to perhaps the most critical set of military reforms in army history during the first decade of the twentieth century. Starting in 1905, Elihu Root, under the reforming guidance of President Theodore Roosevelt, undertook a grand reordering of the army, turning it from a frontier army to one that would be well prepared to expand and fight in mass, industrialized warfare. Ironically, the frontier army, which had spent a generation fighting in the American West, and found itself in a similar situation in the Philippines, would not long outlast the military forces it defeated there. The Philippines were, for the army, the end of the frontier.[23]

The navy went through a similar process after the Civil War. What had been among the most powerful navies in the world in 1865 began to disappear even before the conflict ended. The Confederate naval threat had essentially ended in 1864, and by late 1865 Secretary of the Navy Gideon Welles had reduced the navy's 671 wartime ships by half. The navy remained that size for several years as Welles—in a move of somewhat dubious legality—used funds he had hoarded during the war to sustain the navy afterward. In 1867 the U.S. Navy had more than twice the number of ships in commission as it had in 1860, before the Civil War started.

But there was little political interest in continuing to have a large navy. After 1871, when the Treaty of Washington had settled outstanding claims with Great Britain over their building and sale of commerce raiders to the Confederates, the U.S. Navy, Congress decided, needed to be "respectable, powerful, and efficient," as New Hampshire Congressman Aaron Stevens put it. That did not mean the same thing as it would have meant to the Europeans. Stevens went on: "I do not speak of a British navy or of a French navy; I speak of an American Navy as it has been to our fathers, and such as it should be to us in time of peace."[24]

The result was an American navy that gradually shrank through the 1870s and 1880s. The focus for this smaller navy was on the brown-water strategy of protecting America's coastlines through fortifications and the use of heavily armed but small and short-ranged ships called monitors. Such a combination pleased a parsimonious Congress because it allowed them to disburse money to both the army (for the coastal fortifications) and the navy (for the monitors), thus staving off interservice squabbles. Even more important, the fortifications and ports for the ships brought money to the home states and districts of Congressmen from both coasts, a consideration that always carried great weight.

The only offensive capability the navy retained was a few commerce raiders, following in the footsteps of John Paul Jones and the Confederate *Alabama*. In case of war, they would set to sea and, avoiding other warships, prey upon the merchant ships of the enemy nation. The Monroe Doctrine—though no one said this too explicitly—would be enforced, as it always had been, by the British navy. The United States could be confident of continuing peace with Britain, for that country faced a difficult strategic conundrum in any potential conflict with the United States. Britain's navy greatly overawed that of the United States and would undoubtedly carry the fight to American shores early on, as it had in the War of 1812. But Canada was always vulnerable to American land attack, and there was little that the British could do to protect her. The British army was too small and too committed elsewhere, especially in India, to mount a serious defense. Should war with the United States come, the British would lose Canada, of that they had no doubt. Thus, the British decided, war with the United States could not come. American recognition and use of that was perhaps the most underappreciated diplomatic fact of the nineteenth century.

This began to change in the mid-1880s. The enormous empires of the European powers, particularly of Britain and France, and their massive spending on navies, made the United States begin to suspect that its coastal fortifications were not quite the impenetrable walls it had thought. The result was that Congress hesitantly began to authorize several new classes of ships. In addition, the administration of Grover Cleveland began to lay the foundation for naval construction by organizing the creation of industries and firms that could build large iron ships.

These actions coincided with an intellectual revolution in naval ideas fomented by Adm. Stephen Luce and, more importantly, his protégé Alfred Thayer Mahan. The latter's

The Influence of Sea Power upon History, published in 1890, had a profound effect on global ideas about the uses and needs of naval power. Mahan saw the oceans as great highways of trade and commerce and argued that whoever controlled those oceans controlled the world. The British and French—perhaps unsurprisingly—leaped upon this idea as making concrete what they had been attempting to do all along.

But two others also leaped aboard Mahan's bandwagon, and the results in both cases had enormous long-term consequences. The first was imperial Germany. Kaiser Wilhelm II found in Mahan the prophet he wished to hear, speaking words that would lead to German naval triumph. He had Mahan's book translated into German immediately, and ordered copies for the libraries of every ship in the German navy. He also began the process of creating a great navy for Germany, one that he hoped would rival that of his grandmother, Queen Victoria of England. In so doing, he cast aside the aging Otto von Bismarck, the architect of German unification, and set Germany on a path that would lead to the catastrophic events of 1914.

Also surprisingly, the United States adopted a Mahanian agenda. That Mahan was American may have had something to do with it, but there were other factors as well. The increasing division of the world amongst the great powers, highlighted by the Berlin Conference of 1885, which partitioned Africa, certainly had its effect. But there was also a growing attitude shift on the part of many Americans, both ordinary and elite. The frontier in the West was closed, overrun by railway lines. Manifest destiny had been manifested, and the United States was now largely unrivaled on the North American continent. Its replacement was a continuing sense of American exceptionalism, and one of the representations of that exceptionalism was the impetus to build a navy worthy of the United States. Theodore Roosevelt wrote to Mahan in May 1890 that "I can say with perfect sincerity that I think [your book] very much the clearest and most instructive general work of the kind. . . . I wish . . . that the whole book could be placed where it could be read by the navy's foes, especially in Congress."[25]

This belief was, to a certain degree, independent of Mahan's writing. Before the book was published, President Benjamin Harrison called, in his 1889 inaugural address, for the United States to build "a sufficient number of modern war ships." Sufficient for what, or how many that was, he left to the imagination.[26] But later that same year, Secretary of the Navy Benjamin Tracy asked Congress to authorize a fleet of battleships that could sail the globe and match one-on-one any other ship in the world. Tracy envisioned a fleet of twenty battleships, twelve for the Atlantic and eight for the Pacific. "Until the United States has a fleet of twenty battleships, the country cannot consider that it possesses a Navy; and a Navy it can never afford to be without."[27] Congress agreed, and the 1890 construction program authorized the building of the *Indiana*, *Massachusetts*, and *Oregon*. These battleships were equal to anything in the British navy, and they were the first step in a long process that would see the U.S. Navy supplant the British in the middle of the twentieth century.

In addition to the building program, the United States became increasingly concerned by a strategic problem. The Atlantic and Pacific coasts were separated from each other by thousands of miles of oceans. A battleship could not travel by railroad, and the route southward, around the tip of South America, was a difficult passage that, at best, required months of travel time. The possibility of shortening that journey by thousands of miles by creating a canal across the narrowest part of Central America became an increasingly popular idea among American politicians and strategists. But such a canal would require defense from both European and Asian threats. That defense would have to consist, Mahan insisted, of a larger navy, and of naval bases that could house that navy in a position to protect a canal. Mahan believed that Cuba and the Hawaiian Islands would be particularly useful in this regard.[28]

Two crises convinced the Harrison administration of the rightness of its approach. First, in 1889, a tense standoff developed between German, British, and American warships in the waters around the island of Samoa while their respective governments squabbled over ownership. The crisis brought into relief the critical nature of naval power. Second, in 1891, a confrontation with Chile took place over the jailing of thirty-six American sailors on shore leave in Valparaiso. The sailors, off the cruiser *Baltimore*, had gotten involved in a riot and been arrested. President Harrison demanded their freedom and recompense, but had to back down when it became clear that the Chilean navy could overmatch the American navy. There was even a minor panic on the West Coast that Chilean ships would attack the continental United States. In the end a compromise was worked out.

Though both of these situations were resolved without resorting to military action, both cases—and especially the confrontation with Chile—demonstrated to the administration the need for maintaining and increasing the naval capability of the United States. In his State of the Union

address of December 1891, Benjamin Harrison outlined
that vision, glowingly and in Mahanian terms:

> There should be no hesitation in promptly completing a
> navy of the best modern type, large enough to enable
> this country to display its flag in all seas for the protec-
> tion of its citizens and of its extending commerce. . . .
> It is essential to the dignity of this nation and to that
> peaceful influence which it should exercise on this hemi-
> sphere that its navy should be adequate, both upon the
> shores of the Atlantic and of the Pacific.[29]

By the end of Harrison's term, the U.S. Navy had built
sixteen steam-powered iron warships, and Harrison could
proudly display them in a parade through New York Harbor in April 1893.

This new navy fit well with an increasingly external-
minded and assertive America. That had not been true for
several decades after the Civil War. The effort of that conflict had exhausted most military ambitions on the part of
ordinary Americans. After 1865, the nation's focus was
largely on Reconstruction, both Southern and Northern,
and on the continuing expansion of the country to the
west. By the middle of the 1870s, the immediate task of rebuilding had been accomplished, and the reintegration of
the former Confederate states had been achieved, if incom-
pletely and with grave injustices to the African-American
population. The United States could look forward to progress, modernity, prosperity.

Things were, of course, not that easy. The period from
1877 to 1893 saw the most intense period of an American
economic revolution, and the economy was remade from a

rural and agrarian one to an urban and industrialized one. The transition was chaotic and painful, marked by sudden slumps and bursts of inflation. Even as the size and power of the American economy grew, hundreds of thousands of workers lost jobs in industries that were no longer viable. Migration into cities broke down long-standing social and cultural arrangements and made many Americans strangers to one another. A flood of immigration from Europe and Asia brought millions of new residents into the country, often resented by those born in America, and frequently finding it difficult to adjust to the New World.

When Grover Cleveland took office again in 1893 (having been president from 1885 to 1889), the Democrat slowed down but did not stop the naval building program. Cleveland believed, and had believed in his first term, that the United States needed a strong navy for coastal defense. But he did not share the Mahanian belief that such a navy also required bases outside the continent, and he did not believe that the United States should join in the larger global race for empires. He demonstrated that conviction from the very beginning of his second term by withdrawing a treaty for the annexation of Hawaii that had been submitted to the Senate by Benjamin Harrison in one of his last acts. That decision was made easier by the deeply shady nature of the annexation: a revolution in January of 1893 had deposed the native queen of the islands and replaced her with a government led by white planters, who promptly petitioned to join the United States. Worse, the revolution had been aided by the American government's representative in Hawaii, John L. Stevens, who had illegally used marines from the USS *Boston* to aid the revolutionaries. Cleveland said to Congress in December 1893 that

> if a feeble but friendly state is in danger of being robbed
> of its independence and its sovereignty by a misuse of
> the name and power of the United States, the United
> States cannot fail to vindicate its honor and its sense
> of justice by an earnest effort to make all possible repa-
> ration.[30]

He found, however, that few in Congress agreed with him,
and while he could withhold the treaty from Senate approval, he could not restore the native government.

Cleveland had another reason for being wary about military spending and a gaze focused abroad. Shortly after his
second inauguration, the United States had plunged into
one of the worst depressions in its history. In May 1893 the
economy, overextended after its radical reshaping, without a
financial system that could truly handle its new form, and
feeling the effect of a decades-long agricultural slump, spun
and sputtered to a halt. Hundreds of banks failed and hundreds of thousands of workers were thrown out of jobs.

The depression that ensued was marked by a large
amount of labor unrest as companies drastically cut back
their spending and workers and their nascent labor unions
fought back. Violence was common on both sides. Perhaps
the most famous outbreak was during the Pullman strike of
1894, in which workers on the Pullman railroad company
protested a pay cut that, after they had paid the rent on
company housing, left them with little or nothing for food
and other necessities. The strike became a national cause
when Eugene Debs, eager to enlarge the size and power of
the unions, brought his American Railway Union and its
150,000 members out in sympathy. The resulting strike affected the railroads nationwide and threatened further to

cripple the American economy if not halted. Cleveland, although somewhat sympathetic to the plight of the railroad workers, did not let that stop him from using army troops and court injunctions to protect the railroads. The strike ended with Debs in jail (studying Karl Marx) and the railroad owners triumphant.

The end of the strike was not the end of the depression. Though the worst of it was over by the summer of 1894, the effects continued through 1895–96 and heavily influenced the presidential election of 1896. That race pitted William Jennings Bryan, a Democratic candidate supported largely by agrarian interests in the West and the Solid South, against William McKinley, a Republican supported by the industrial interests of the Northeast, Midwest, and Pacific coast. Bryan's great failing was his inability to appeal to the industrial workers of the big cities, a constituency that should have been a natural ally given his perceived radicalism. He lost the election to the quiet McKinley.

Two

MCKINLEY AND
AMERICAN IMPERIALISM

Though William McKinley has been seen as something of a nonentity, a front for business interests controlled by his campaign manager Mark Hanna, the real picture is much more complex. McKinley knew his mind and ran his presidency as he wished, though he normally displayed a stoic face to the public. At first, McKinley's foreign and military policies echoed those of Cleveland's. In his inaugural address, he remarked that the United States "cherished the policy of non-interference with affairs of foreign governments," and that such should continue, for "we want no wars of conquest; we must avoid the temptation of territorial aggression."[1]

McKinley followed those words by appointing the elderly and resolutely calm John D. Long to the office of secretary of the navy, a signal that while the building of warships might continue, their aggressive use would not. How much of this expressed McKinley's own moderate views and how much was simply a ritualistic bow to the long American tradition of noninterference in foreign affairs is not clear. What is clear is that from the very start, McKinley matched his soothing words with aggressive actions. One of the first of these was the appointment of Theodore Roosevelt as assistant secretary of the navy, under Long. Roosevelt was Mahanian to his core, and aggressive. "Too pugnacious?" McKinley wondered. Perhaps, but that pugnacity would usefully balance the staid Long.[2]

In addition, almost immediately after being inaugurated, McKinley reversed Cleveland's policy on Hawaii. The government that had taken over the islands in 1893 had remained relatively stable over the ensuing years, and McKinley, in the summer of 1897, negotiated and signed a treaty of annexation with that government. Hawaii would join the United States and provide a valuable stepping-stone to the markets of Asia. The annexation would also act to curtail growing Japanese interest in the islands. But McKinley's prospects of getting the treaty ratified by the Senate were bleak. Though the Republicans held a small majority, they did not have much chance of summoning the two-thirds necessary for ratification.

Before a confrontation in the Senate could occur, a crisis erupted that would dominate McKinley's first term: the revolution in Cuba. The situation there resembled the situation in the Philippines in many ways. It was an outpost of a largely vanished Spanish empire, economically backward and dominated by a small Spanish elite. Just as in the Philippines, a revolution started. But the insurgency in

Cuba was much more organized and more effective than the fragmentary one in the Philippines.

The Spanish found themselves losing. Unable to buy off the leaders of the revolt, they resorted to harsher and harsher measures to try to control the situation. The governor-general of Cuba, Valeriano Weyler, instituted measures known as the *reconcentrado*, which included concentrating the civilian population into areas where they could be controlled by the Spanish army. The army found it enormously difficult to keep these civilians fed, and the starvation of thousands of Cubans was widely reported in the United States. In addition, a number of American citizens on the island were mistreated or threatened by Spanish forces. In combination, these things, agitated by the American press, led to a growing animosity toward Spain amongst broad sections of the American public.

The situation was made worse for the Spanish because the emperor of Spain, Alfonso XIII, was twelve years old. His mother, Maria Cristina, was the regent, but another member of the royal family, Don Carlos, also claimed the throne. In 1897 Carlos was in exile, but there were strong factions within Spain which would have welcomed his return. Any capitulation on Cuba would likely have led to open revolution in Spain. The Spanish were, in essence, trapped politically and militarily. They were not winning the war in Cuba, but domestic concerns made it nearly impossible to pull out.

In the summer of 1897 McKinley prodded the Spanish government, instructing the new ambassador to Madrid, Steward Lyndon Woodford, to ask the king whether "Spain has not already had a reasonable time to restore peace and has been unable to do so." This "inability entails upon the

United States a degree of injury and suffering which can not longer be ignored." The ambassador was instructed to say however that the only goal of the United States was to find "a peaceful and enduring result . . . just and honorable alike to Spain and to the Cuban people." Nonetheless, McKinley reminded the Spanish, the situation was urgent enough that the United States would have to reach "an early decision as to the course of action which the time and the transcendent emergency may demand."[3]

McKinley's delicate verbal balancing act drew results. The Spanish government recalled Weyler and offered autonomy to the Cuban revolutionaries: not independence, but self-government under a Spanish version of benign neglect. The Cubans, who sensed the weakness of Spain and the growing interest of the United States, refused. It was to be *Cuba Libre* or nothing at all.

McKinley might well have extended his negotiations for a long time. In December he reiterated his wish to use "peaceful agencies" to resolve the situation.[4] In addition to his own personal beliefs, the business interests that had done so much to get McKinley elected were deeply ambivalent about a war with Spain. But a catastrophe intervened. The battleship *Maine*, sent to Cuba after riots in Havana threatened American property, blew up on the night of February 15, 1898, killing most of its crew.

Reaction to the explosion in the United States was immediate and fierce. William Randolph Hearst, the newspaper proprietor, said, immediately upon hearing the news, "This means war!" The newspapers and the public blamed Spanish sabotage. A court of inquiry was immediately convened to probe the explosion. The investigation took more than a month, and in that period war fever in the United

States surged. McKinley's wait for the results of the inquiry came to be seen as spinelessness, and his popularity began to slip. Charles Dawes, the controller of the currency and one of McKinley's closest advisers, wrote of the "abuse" and "awful pressure" heaped on the president by the papers. When Wall Street slid down upon the prospect of war, the press turned on it, calling the New York financial interests "the colossal and aggregate Benedict Arnold of the Union and the syndicated Judas Iscariot of humanity."[5]

When the court finally reported its conclusion that the ship had been "destroyed by the explosion of a submarine mine" by a person or persons unknown, war became inevitable. On April 11 McKinley sent a message to Congress recommending military intervention in Cuba, although even that was, as Dawes put it, "too judicial and too just to suit those who are for war at any price." On April 20 Congress passed a joint resolution authorizing the use of force, but disclaiming (in the so-called Teller Amendment) any interest in long-term American possession of the island. A declaration of war on Spain followed on April 25, 1898.[6]

To understand how the Philippines reappear in this story requires understanding the dynamics within the Navy Department. The elderly and infirm secretary of the navy, John Long, was prone to a range of chronic digestive troubles. He was often overwhelmed by his youthful and energetic assistant secretary, Theodore Roosevelt. In 1896 a young officer in the Navy Department, Lt. Warren Kimball, had designed a war plan in case of conflict with Spain. The plan included major actions in the Caribbean, but it also postulated sending the U.S. Asiatic fleet—a collection of armored cruisers based in Hong Kong—against Spanish ships in the Philippines.

Pursuant to that plan, Roosevelt acted to ensure that the Asiatic fleet was led by an aggressive and thrusting commander. He chose Commodore George Dewey, who had impressed him during the crisis with Chile. Political maneuvering in September 1897 while Secretary Long was out of the office got Dewey appointed to the command over Long's preferred candidate, the more passive Commodore John Howell. Long returned from his vacation to find a letter from McKinley asking for Dewey's appointment. He could hardly overrule the president.

Dewey had not particularly distinguished himself until the Chilean crisis. Growing up in Vermont, he had been an adequate student, and had won admittance to the Naval Academy only as an alternate in 1854. Dewey made little mark at Annapolis. He finished fifth in his class of fourteen. During the Civil War he served adequately under Admiral Farragut. But along with all other naval officers, he faced stagnation in the post–Civil War years. Perhaps his most important move in those postwar years was getting married to Susan Goodwin, the daughter of the Republican governor of New Hampshire, in 1867. Unfortunately Susan Goodwin Dewey died soon after childbirth, leaving Dewey with a son, George, Jr., to raise.

It is perhaps cynical to see his marriage simply as a career move to help him advance in the navy, although according to his sister he "felt as if in no little measure his career had ended at the grave of his wife."[7] Now, at Roosevelt's behest, Dewey had been given what would turn out to be perhaps the most important American naval command in the years between 1865 and 1941.

When the crisis with Spain erupted, Roosevelt was thus prepared. On February 25, 1898, Long was absent from the office because of illness, and Roosevelt seized the opportunity to send a telegram to Dewey, ordering the Asiatic fleet to Hong Kong and telling the commodore that, upon declaration of war with Spain, he should attack the Spanish fleet in the Philippines.

This was grossly outside of Roosevelt's authority as assistant secretary. When Long returned the next day and discovered what Roosevelt had done, he complained that "in my short absence, I find that Roosevelt . . . has come very near causing more of an explosion than happened to the *Maine*."[8] Long wished in his heart of hearts that the United States could remain "provincial," an agrarian nation safe behind its ocean walls. But he did not believe he could stop the "march of events—a march which seems to be beyond human control."[9] Thus, fatalistically, he did not countermand Roosevelt's orders, and so Dewey moved the fleet to Hong Kong, provisioned himself with coal and supplies, and waited, the Philippines in his gaze.

It is here that Aguinaldo reappears. Aguinaldo had been traveling in the spring of 1898, in large part to avoid a lawsuit in Hong Kong. On his return he stopped in Singapore and met with the American consul there, E. Spencer Pratt. The resulting conversation has remained shrouded in controversy. Aguinaldo insisted that Pratt promised American support for Filipino independence, that the consul wooed him with "honeyed phrases and Old-World courtesies."[10] Pratt just as strongly denied that he had promised anything. The only witness was their translator, an Englishman named Howard Bray. Bray backed up Aguinaldo. The Englishman, however, had been promised money and a job by the Filipino leader, opening his testimony to some doubt. Aguinaldo did not make it to Hong Kong before

Dewey left, but when he arrived, he was loaded onto an American ship and sent in the fleet's wake.

The Battle of Manila Bay

It was not the right season for naval operations in the South China Sea. Monsoons blowing from the southwest made sailing difficult for all but the largest vessels. To make things worse, when Dewey arrived in Hong Kong, he found that an outbreak of the bubonic plague was sweeping through the city, killing thousands.

The commodore nonetheless anchored, ordered his white ships painted gray for battle, and set forth on April 27 with a force of seven modern warships, led by the armored cruiser *Olympia* and including the cruisers *Baltimore*, *Raleigh*, and *Boston*, the gunboats *Concord* and *Petrel*, and the revenue cutter *McCulloch*. It did not seem like a large or imposing force to the British officers stationed in Hong Kong. They had liked the Americans: "A fine set of fellows, but unhappily we shall never see them again."[11]

There were three reporters hitching a ride on the *McCulloch*, Edwin Harden of the *New York World*, Joseph Stickney of the *New York Herald*, and John McCutcheon of the *Chicago Record*. Though not as pessimistic as the British officers, they were nonetheless worried: "For Harden, Stickney, and myself," wrote McCutcheon, "it seemed like we would be sailing into the jaws of a dragon. . . . Fearing the worst, we wrote farewell letters home. . . ."[12]

The Americans, to make matters worse, had to give battle quickly. They had two supply ships with them, but that was not nearly enough for a lengthy campaign. Without a local base, and during a season in which monsoons and typhoons were frequent, Dewey could not risk staying at sea for long.

When Dewey arrived at the Philippines on April 30, he was unsure of the location of the Spanish fleet. He sent a ship to investigate Subic Bay, to the north of Manila. Subic proved to be empty; Dewey concluded that the Spanish were sheltering in Manila Bay. He contemplated his course of action. There were dangers in the bay besides the Spanish ships. The Spanish would surely have mined the waters, and the island of Corregidor, which bisected the entry channel, was fortified with artillery emplacements. In such confined waters Dewey's force might suffer heavily. But he had his old Civil War mentor to remember and decades of little action behind him:

> I have waited sixty years for this opportunity. Mines or no mines, I am leading the squadron in myself. . . . I confess, I was thinking of [Admiral Farragut] the night we entered Manila Bay and with the conviction that I was doing precisely what he would have done.[13]

The commodore decided to push ahead and beard the Spanish lion in its den. Upon entering the bay, however, Dewey found the threats less than he expected. There were no mines, and the artillery on Corregidor was poorly handled. In addition, the ships that faced Dewey were massively inferior to his own. The seven Spanish vessels matched the Americans in number, but little else. They were antiquated, unarmored warships that presented no real threat to the American fleet. The Spanish had anchored off Cavite, a fortified point directly across from Manila city. There, protected by the artillery on Cavite, the Spanish would make their stand. The Spanish admiral, realizing the vulnerability of his ships, had deliberately anchored in shallow water, so that his sailors would have more chance to struggle ashore if their craft went down.

The next morning, May 1, Dewey methodically set about destroying the Spanish fleet. The Spanish sailors and officers fought gallantly, but their guns had difficulty reaching the American ships and could not penetrate the armor when they did. By contrast, the American guns wrecked the Spanish ships. The battle lasted most of the day. By the time it had ended, the entire Spanish fleet had been sunk, with the loss of over four hundred men. John McCutcheon remembered the scene:

> At dark, the shores around Cavite glowed bright with the flames of burning ships. The *Reina Cristina* and *Castilla* [two of the Spanish ships] looked like skeletons. The fires consuming them made their bones appear black against the white-hot heat. In the flickering light, the devastation at Cavite took on a surrealistic look— like the gateway to Hades. Occasionally an ammunition magazine would erupt like a volcano, throwing its flaming debris high in the air, making a grisly picture of the horrors of modern warfare.[14]

"The magnificent fleets of Spain," wrote one newspaper at home, "have gone down as marvelously . . . as the walls of Jericho went down."[15]

By contrast, the American fleet lost no ships, had no sailors killed, and only a few wounded. In hindsight, given the disparity in forces, it was not surprising that the Americans had won. But at the time the victory created a deep impression, not only on the Spanish but on other European powers. It was a symbolic victory: the upstart American nation routing a great if decaying European empire. In that brief battle, Dewey had shown the United States to be a world power, one that demanded attention and respect.

Dewey's telegram home neatly summarized the situation: "Not one Spanish flag flies in Manila Bay today; not one Spanish warship floats except as our prize."[16] The news of the battle was received in the United States on May 7. It electrified a country awash with war fever but frightened of the possibility of a Spanish attack on the East Coast. Dewey's victory was a tonic for a country nervously if enthusiastically involved in its first major external war since 1848. Dewey overnight became the most popular man in America, immortalized on everything from paperweights to cigarettes. Cities put up statues of the hero, and merchants did a brisk trade in Dewey photographs for the home. On May 10 the commodore was promoted to rear admiral as a reward. It was the overreaction of a country aching to place itself in the front rank of powers and eager to compare itself in might to its old colonial master, Great Britain. "England had her Sir Francis Drake, her Lord Howe, her Rodney and Lord Nelson. . . . [Dewey's] name is destined to be wreathed with [the same] immortal glory," wrote one biographer in 1898.[17]

Dewey and the American fleet were left the essential masters of the Philippines. They controlled Manila Bay and the waters around the archipelago. There was no prospect of another Spanish fleet arriving. All her naval reinforcements were on the way to Cuba, and further disaster. The Spanish army in Manila, consisting of roughly 20,000 men, could do nothing except threaten Dewey's ships with obsolete coastal artillery. Dewey controlled the bay, the entrepôt of the Philippines, and thus controlled the economy of the archipelago. Even worse for the Spanish, they soon had to deal with a reinvigorated insurgent army. Emilio Aguinaldo arrived in the Philippines on May 19, ready to resume the revolution.

Upon arrival, he met with Dewey. As with his talk with Pratt, the resulting conversation was forever after reported differently by different parties. Aguinaldo claimed that Dewey also promised the Philippines independence; Dewey denied saying any such thing.[18] Dewey, of course, did not have the authority to make such a promise—though given the propensity of many to exceed their authority, notably Roosevelt, perhaps this is not a convincing argument.

In any case, it does not matter. Aguinaldo certainly had an interest, then and later, in representing whatever Dewey and Pratt said as a guarantee that the Philippines would be given independence. Dewey and Pratt for their parts wished for Aguinaldo's support against the Spanish, but certainly knew that they had no chance of making any such assurance stick if the American government decided otherwise. They might have lied to Aguinaldo; they might have implied to Aguinaldo; they might have done neither. But whatever the full extent of the conversation, the immediate result was an informal alliance between the Philippine *insurrectos* and the United States, similar to the one between the United States and the Cuban insurrectos.

The one concrete and lasting thing that Aguinaldo did get out of Dewey was equipment. The commodore gave Aguinaldo one hundred rifles immediately and had the American consul in Hong Kong purchase a few thousand more. Such weapons helped remedy the most critical short-

coming of the revolutionary army and ensured that
Aguinaldo—whatever the skepticism about the Treaty of
Biak-na-Bato—would be welcomed back by his Filipino
comrades. Within a few weeks a reinvigorated Filipino
army was again waging war against the Spanish. Aguinaldo
organized his forces to include both regular troops, those
with experience and equipment, and a revolutionary militia
consisting of everyone else. They were soon besieging isolated Spanish garrisons outside Manila and moving on the
city itself.[19]

In addition, Aguinaldo began organizing a Filipino government. On June 23, 1898, he issued a proclamation laying out the form of the new government. He built his
structure on the existing municipal councils. They would
elect assemblies for each province, which, in turn, would
elect a governor. Finally, each province would send two or
three representatives to a gathering that would write a new
constitution for the archipelago. The vote, in all cases,
was strictly limited to those with substantial property hold-
ings. On top of the whole structure was the president—
Aguinaldo—who was the "personification of the Philippine
people," with a term that would "last until the revolution
triumphs."[20] Aguinaldo and his allies were not interested in
mass democracy, but an elite republic, controlled by the
privileged and by Aguinaldo.

Acquiring the Islands

For McKinley, Dewey's victory presented problems. What,
exactly, should he do? One response would be to send
troops to defeat the Spanish army and occupy at least
Manila. The forces for that contingency were training at the

Presidio base in San Francisco. Thousands of volunteer soldiers suffered there from the cold spring winds blowing off the ocean, the rigorous physical training put in place by Gen. Elwell Otis, and diseases caused by inadequate sanitary facilities. It was an odd force, composed of units hastily and irregularly raised and funded. For example, John Jacob Astor, the wealthy New Yorker, had opened his checkbook and promised funding for a unit of artillery. The so-called Astor Battery was put together by Lt. Peyton March, future chief of staff of the army, out of a set of guns purchased by telegram from Paris, a set of uniforms made of British khaki courtesy of a New York clothing firm, and volunteers from the Ivy League universities.[21]

But sending troops to the Philippines went far beyond the strategic plan that had sent Dewey's ships to Manila Bay. The Spanish fleet there presented a potential threat to the American West Coast. Destroying it as part of a campaign to liberate Cuba was a reasonable defensive maneuver to cover America's flanks. But stepping beyond that strategy and grabbing the islands themselves was an entirely different thing.

McKinley officially decided to put off the decision regarding the final disposition of the Philippines. But in reality he moved the nation closer to seizing them by ordering the War Department to send troops. On May 25, 1898, Brig. Gen. Thomas Anderson, a Civil War veteran, and roughly 2,500 men and officers from the First California, Second Oregon, and U.S. Fourteenth Infantry regiments boarded ships to take them to Manila. With them was sent a geologist, to evaluate the natural resources of the archipelago. Cheering crowds thronged the streets of San Francisco to see the troops off.

The trip was not as pleasant as the departure. Crammed into freighters, the soldiers suffered from disease, seasickness, and insect infestation. The army had equipped the ships with delousers, but the machines apparently destroyed clothing as well as bugs, leaving a number of soldiers without any underwear.[22] Theodore Wurm, a private in the Eighteenth U.S. Regiment, remembered:

> [We] soon got out in the Pacific and it proved rather rough. Everyone got sick the first night and plenty of water got into the port holes before being closed. The odor caused from the thousand sea sick vomiting [men] was very bad. Very few could eat or cared to see others do so.[23]

The force stopped off at Honolulu to resupply, then sailed to the Spanish possession of Guam. Upon arriving there the escorting cruiser, the *Charleston*, fired shots over the Spanish fort. The Spanish commander—who had not gotten word of the war between the two nations—rowed out apologetically. He had no cannon to return what he presumed was a salute. The Americans brought him up to date and occupied the island before continuing on to the Philippines.

This force was followed by two others, one of approximately 3,550 officers and men under Brig. Gen. Francis Greene, which left San Francisco on June 15, and one of about 4,800 officers and men under Brig. Gen. Arthur MacArthur, accompanied by the overall commander, Gen. Wesley Merritt, which left on June 27.

General Merritt was experienced. He had graduated from West Point in 1860, had fought valiantly in the Civil

War, and had reached the rank of brevet major general by its end. In the thirty years that followed he had fought in the West in the nearly unending series of Indian Wars. By 1898, he was, in all ways, a veteran. But while he—and his officers—had a great deal of experience in war, they had no experience and little knowledge of the Philippines. Indeed, the American officers, as Arthur MacArthur later remembered, had an "absolute ignorance" of the islands. And the information they received did not do much to alleviate that: "One writer to whom we had access" MacArthur continued, "advised all travelers to carry coffins, as few returned alive from Manila."[24]

Upon arrival the soldiers were billeted in the Spanish naval barracks on Cavite. Offshore were the hulks of the Spanish fleet sunk by Dewey, and from those hulks rose bubbles filled by the gases of decaying Spanish corpses. The smell that came ashore was pungent and omnipresent. In addition, it was the rainy season in the Philippines, making it difficult to light a fire in the near-constant rain. Though the soldiers did not have to keep warm in tropical Manila, they did need to boil their drinking water to make it potable. Without a fire, that was not possible. Potentially worse, the coffee beans issued by the quartermaster were green, and without a fire to roast them the soldiers risked going without coffee. They were confident though, despite the problems. As William Christner of the Tenth Pennsylvania put it, the soldiers "intended to take [Manila] and put it in our pockets."[25]

The political and military situation was complicated. The Spanish garrison in Manila was cut off by Dewey's ships from supply or reinforcement. The stranglehold got tighter as American troops arrived. The Army of Liberation, as the Filipinos called their forces, had surrounded the city with roughly 13,000 to 15,000 men. Inside the old city of Manila, a similar number of Spanish troops faced them, along with anywhere between 50,000 and 70,000 civilians. Food and other necessities were in short supply. On Cavite were the American troops.

Technically, the Americans and the insurgents were allies against the Spanish, but both sides expressed a certain amount of suspicion of each other, at levels high and low. Aguinaldo publicly professed a sunny certainty of the benign nature of American motives. In July 1898 he said in a meeting with American officers, "I have studied attentively the Constitution of the United States and in it I find no authority for colonies and I have no fear."[26] But in private, many of the Filipino leaders suspected the Americans. They found it hard to believe that the United States would not "covet this very beautiful pearl of the Orient Sea."[27]

On the American side, the generals did not think much of the insurgents, either. The second in command, Gen. Elwell Otis, offered an evaluation that many officers shared. Aguinaldo's army, he thought, was made up of "all the robbers of the island of Luzon," whose goal was to "kill every white man in Manila." His view of Filipinos in general was similarly uncharitable: he thought them "ignorant and very superstitious."[28]

Nor were ordinary soldiers particularly impressed with the insurgents. Theodore Wurm wrote in his diary:

> The Insurgent is a very poor appearing soldier—They go about the very narrow and dirty streets at will with their arms. Saw Mauser and Remington Rifles and large knives of any design probably waiting to be called for

duty. No system seems to be established among them. The men are small but generously well built and muscular and the majority are in need of arms. They are trying to buy any kind of fire arms from us and are offering high prices. Nearly all the natives go without shoes and their clothing is scant and of very light weight material.[29]

Merritt was determined, per McKinley's orders, that the Americans would be the ones to take Manila by themselves, without Filipino participation. But how? They had to get American troops ashore near Manila so that they could mount an assault on the city without going through the insurgent lines. Merritt did not wish to use force against the insurgents and end up fighting two armies at once.

The break came in personal negotiations between General Greene and one of his counterparts in the Philippine forces, Gen. Mariano Noriel. Greene persuaded the Filipino to allow the American forces to occupy a portion of Noriel's left wing, from the beach that led into Manila Bay to an inland swamp. As fighting territory, it was dismal. The American trenches filled with water almost immediately, and the mosquitoes, large and hungry in the swamp, took their toll on American hides. The Spanish position opposite was particularly strong, anchored by two large blockhouses. But the American line was anchored on the left by Manila Bay, which allowed the navy to both supply the troops and support them with gunfire.

Once the Americans were ashore, the three forces rubbed elbows somewhat uneasily. Aguinaldo was becoming increasingly suspicious of the Americans, and the Americans were trying to figure out how to occupy Manila without allowing the insurgents inside as well. In the end it was the Spanish who provided a way. In early August, Governor-General Augustin sent a telegram to Spain asking for permission to surrender. The reply instead relieved him and put his second in command, General Jaudenes, in charge. But the new governor-general agreed with Augustin that the situation was hopeless, so he negotiated through the Belgian consul with Admiral Dewey. The result of that negotiation was, if not a complete surrender, at least an agreement that, when the Americans attacked, Spanish resistance would cease as soon as honor permitted. One observer remarked of the agreement and the resulting battle, "The tragedy lost its tragic character and became a comedy before the performance began, and the performance itself developed into pretty nearly a farce."[30]

Merritt mounted an assault on August 13, sending the American forces into the Spanish lines across from them, supported by the guns of Dewey's ships. The main points of attack were Fort San Antonio Abad near the beach and Blockhouse 14 a few hundred yards inland. Both fell relatively quickly. Theodore Wurm wrote of the assault several days later in his diary:

> The greatest obstacle to overcome was in getting over the ground and ahead, the way leading over wire fences and rice and cane fields which in places was nearly impassable, the ground being covered with water to the depth of a foot or more and as much more mud underneath. A continual fire of small arms was kept up by the enemy and the bullets were [splashing] in the water under foot and too near to make one feel comfortable. No determined resistance was made by the enemy after the

Fleet dislodged them from their intrenchments. It was a rout.[31]

Within hours the American soldiers had secured the Spanish fortifications and accepted the surrender of the rest of the Spanish forces. But what resistance there was slowed the Americans enough so that the Filipino insurgents learned of the attack and advanced into the suburbs of Manila. They were stopped from reaching the city proper by American troops in confrontations that edged toward violence. Nonetheless, by the end of the day, the Eighth Corps controlled Manila and had managed to exclude the Filipinos from any part in that possession. One of the soldiers, Private Henry King Skilman, wrote home to his mother about the celebration:

> Just as soon as we could pull that Spanish flag down up went the Stars and Stripes, our beloved "Old Glory" and, mother dear, I never felt before like I did at that moment. The tears filled my eyes and I choked up so that I could not shout for a moment, and I knew then what it was that you felt when you told me not to forget for one moment that the most glorious thing in all the world was that same flag, and that it was my first duty to protect it at all hazards. I have not forgotten your glorious words, for the happiest moment in all my life was when I saw that flag on high. You ought to have heard the sailors cheer when it went up—that beautiful banner. . . . the United States is God's country.[32]

With Manila and its bay, the United States possessed the economic heart of the Philippines. Dewey's triumph had been cemented, and, whatever else happened, Spain's power in the Pacific was permanently crippled. The question, of course, was what should the United States do with the Philippines?

What to Do?

The debate at home over exactly that question had been going on with some intensity since Dewey's victory. The Philippines themselves were not particularly well known in the United States. As the historian Richard Hofstadter later pointed out, American media attention to the Philippines in the eighty-year period from 1818 to 1898 could be measured by the number of magazine articles published on them: thirty-five.[33] Despite this lack of knowledge, there was a growing sense that the United States was destined to gain expansively from the war. It was only right, *National Geographic* declared, that the country should "take its rightful position among the nations of the earth. . . . The welfare of our nation lies largely in the development of our trade with the nations south of us and countries of the Far East. . . . Our policy in the future must be an aggressive one."[34]

This expansionist fever had given McKinley a chance to complete the annexation of Hawaii. Getting the Senate to ratify a treaty to take the island chain remained impossible, so McKinley turned to other, somewhat dubious methods. During the late spring and early summer of 1898, he threatened to take Hawaii using his power as commander in chief. Congress capitulated, and passed a joint resolution making Hawaii part of the United States, a resolution that McKinley signed on July 7, 1898. Such a method was not without precedent; the annexation of Texas had been managed by joint resolution in 1845 at the behest of President

John Tyler. Since that annexation had contributed to the sectional divisions underpinning the Civil War, it was perhaps not the best omen for the future.[35]

But what to do with the Philippines? Uncertainty ruled. Even the apostle of naval expansionism, Alfred Thayer Mahan, was confused:

> Personally, I have not yet become wholly adjusted to the new point of view opened to us by Dewey's victory in Manila. It has opened a vista of possibilities which were not by me in the least foreseen. . . . As it is, I look with a kind of awe upon the passage of events in which the will of man seems to count for little.[36]

Nor were the politicians more certain of their ground. There is the sense of an administration that was, to an extent, figuring things out on the fly, especially with regard to the Philippines. On July 28, Charles Dawes, one of McKinley's close political advisers, confided to his diary:

> If we could only be assured that Spain had common sense, peace and a proper Governmental policy would seem in sight. The longer war continues, the greater will be the public demand that we keep all the Philippines, not because they are deemed desirable for us so much as because another course may seem a concession to Spain. As more lives are lost, the greater will be the public desire to keep the Philippines, not so much for themselves as to punish Spain.[37]

There is a plaintive suggestion in Dawes's words of a situation only barely under control.

The situation became more urgent in late July. The Spanish monarchy began to feel that this disastrous war would lead to an internal revolt, and concluded that they should end it quickly. Attempts to get the other great powers to bring pressure on the United States to negotiate failed. Finally, on July 22, the Spanish petitioned the administration directly for an armistice and the opening of peace negotiations. Given the overwhelming American success, that seemed logical to McKinley. But what to ask for? Cuban independence was a given. American acquisition of Puerto Rico and other Spanish islands in the Caribbean was relatively uncontroversial. The accession of an island in the central Pacific chain of the Marianas—most likely Guam— was largely favored. But what to do about the Philippines? Should the administration take nothing, take Manila and Manila Bay, or take the whole thing? At a meeting on July 30 the cabinet agreed—though not without some discussion—to take only the city of Manila and the surrounding area to serve as a naval base and economic hub. The peace negotiators, the cabinet decided, would settle the final status of the islands.

On August 12 the Spanish and American governments signed an armistice ending hostilities, the day before distant Manila fell. The end of combat and the looming peace negotiations made the Philippine question even more critical. Other powers sniffed around the Philippines, wondering perhaps if they could snatch them away from this impudent upstart power. German warships maneuvered threateningly, hovering in the waters around the archipelago and even inside Manila Bay. Their actions after the destruction of the Spanish fleet "began to excite much interest and considerable irritation among the officers and men of the American warships. Admiral Dewey was constantly receiving reports that the Germans were not observing an attitude of strict neutrality."[38] The Germans exacerbated the situation in June by reinforcing their squadron in the South China Sea to such a point that it might have been capable of overwhelming Dewey's should a fight break out. Such behavior by the Germans gave greater weight to the voices advising McKinley that to leave the Philippines after eliminating Spanish power would give other imperial powers—Germany, France, Britain, and Russia—the opening to snatch the archipelago for themselves.

In addition, the Far East was a hotbed of activity, with a range of European powers squabbling over various territories and eyeing covetously the giant prize that was China.[39] The Philippines would serve the United States well as a stepping-stone for influence in the Chinese situation. An American coaling station at Manila or Subic Bay would give the navy the reach it needed to have a strong say in China.

The Naval War Board's report, written by Alfred Thayer Mahan on August 15–20, 1898, made exactly that argument. "The future of China [is] quite the most interesting commercial question of the Pacific to us at the present moment." For that question, "the port of Manila is very centrally situated as regards the whole sweep of the eastern coast of Asia." The report recommended taking Manila (or Subic) Bay and the island of Guam as a transit point to the Philippines.[40]

Other voices chimed in to reinforce the argument.

Dewey recommended that the navy build its base at Subic Bay, as Manila Bay would be hard to defend.[41] In addition, Sen. Henry Cabot Lodge told the president, the Philippines themselves would be a valuable market:

> The time has now come when [the domestic] market is not enough for our teeming industries, and the great demand of the day is an outlet for our products. . . . With our protective tariff wall around the Philippine islands, its ten million inhabitants, as they advance in civilization, would have to buy our goods, and we should have so much additional market for our home manufactures.[42]

Finally, it should be noted that 1898 was a congressional election year, and should McKinley dispose of the Philippines in a way that displeased the American people, the Republicans were likely to suffer at the polls. The mood in the country was decidedly imperialist and expansionist and there was little support for letting the Philippines go. Returning them wholesale to Spain was certainly not an option; after fighting a war to liberate the Cubans from Spanish tyranny, returning the Filipinos to the same tyranny would seem the height of hypocrisy. McKinley was careful to gauge public opinion in the fall of 1898, first by talking to Republican political operatives and then by touring the Midwest and giving speeches to feel out popular opinion. He used the October opening of the Trans-Mississippi and International Exposition in Omaha, Nebraska, as a place to start his tour. Among other things, the exposition offered for spectators a model Philippine village that at one point included sixteen "Manila warriors . . .

with cannibalistic proclivities." What McKinley found was that speaking of America's "divine ordination" by God to assume "international responsibilities" was extremely popular at the local level.[43]

All of these influences pushed McKinley in the direction of taking all of the islands. In November of the following year, he supposedly told a group of Methodist ministers visiting the White House that as he agonized over the question long into the night, God spoke to him and told him to take the Philippines. There are some difficulties with this account. The minister who recounted it, James F. Rousling, waited several years to relate the story, and, as the historian Lewis Gould has pointed out, the story strongly echoed a similar account that Rousling had given of a meeting with Abraham Lincoln after Gettysburg.[44]

In any case, there is less of a sense of a sudden epiphanic decision than a gradual shift in thinking within the administration that it was impossible *not* to take the Philippines. Witness Whitelaw Reid, the Republican editor of the *New York Tribune* and a close confidant of McKinley, as he discussed the archipelago in a July 1898 letter:

> It is extremely doubtful whether [Spain] will be allowed to retain the Philippines—not because we want them, but because our people are so convinced of the cruelty and barbarity of Spanish rule over semi-civilized races, that they would consider themselves guilty of any subsequent cruelty if they remanded these islands to the Spaniards. Probably, if either France or England could take them without stirring up general European difficulties, we should be glad to get rid of them.[45]

The sense of Reid mentally throwing his hands in the air is too strong to ignore. But within two weeks the editor had adjusted his position. Now it was possible that the United States could "hold Manila" and possibly have a protectorate around the rest of the islands. By early October Reid had expanded his ambition again, convinced that "we must retain the whole of them anyway."[46] The archipelago became, for a great many Republicans, up to and including the president, something of an accidental acquisition: a large, unwieldy Christmas gift that, if nice, was also rather difficult to fit into the household.

McKinley's views seem to have evolved in much the same way. Henry Cabot Lodge wrote on August 12 that "McKinley is firm about Cuba and Puerto Rico, but hesitant about what to do in the East."[47] The hesitation continued when McKinley gave his final instructions to the peace commission (which included Whitelaw Reid) before it set off to Paris. He told them to take Manila and the island of Luzon for the United States, but left the question of the other islands open. His Midwestern tour reassured him about the political side of things, however, and by late October he concluded that the United States had to take the Philippines. On October 25 he sent a cable to the commissioners in Paris:

> There is a general feeling in the United States that whatever it might prefer to do, America is in a situation where it cannot let go. The interdependency of the several islands, their proximity to Luzon, the grave problem of what will become of the part we do not take are all being considered by the people. My opinion is that the well considered opinion of the majority believes duty requires we should take the Philippines.[48]

McKinley had decided; now the only question was how the United States would negotiate the acquisition of the Philippines: by simple right of conquest, or by something more involved?

The negotiations in Paris were between a defeated, decadent power and a vibrant young one, and Whitelaw Reid was strongly aware of the distinction. As the negotiators for the United States read out American demands, Reid was struck by the Spanish demeanor:

> It was really a dramatic spectacle, [as] these provisions for deeding away the last vestige of their possessions in the world they had discovered and settled were slowly read. . . . [The Spanish] were all visibly moved; and old Montero looked as a Roman Senator might, when told that the Goths were at the gates.

The Spanish diplomats played the role convincingly at the Paris peace negotiations, whether out of genuine dismay or as a ploy to win better terms is not entirely clear. "You have had a great victory," one of them said to Whitelaw Reid. "Now, you must prove your greatness by your magnanimity."[49]

The scale of the Spanish defeat, however, was simply too large and the internal position of their government too shaky for Spanish negotiators to manage much. Nor could they induce the other powers to come to their assistance. The Spanish begged various powers, including, in a sign of desperation, America's traditional ally Russia, to intervene and get the United States to moderate its demands. It was not to be. Both Britain and Russia refused to get involved, preferring for the Philippines to fall to the Americans rather than to a potential European rival. The Germans, despite their provocations in Manila Bay, also refused to attempt an intervention, though the daughter of the German ambassador did find time to say to Reid that "I was against you in your war. I was on the side of the little dog. Whatever his faults, at any rate I wish he had taken a good bite out of you." Spain's position at the bargaining table worsened in early November when the Republicans suffered only marginal losses in the midterm elections. Theodore Roosevelt, back from a stint in Cuba, pulled out a narrow victory for the governorship of New York. McKinley's position was assured, and that guaranteed little in the way of generosity from the American negotiators.[50]

The result was a treaty, signed on December 10, 1898, that gave the United States everything it wanted. Cuba was independent, although Cuban debt remained with Spain. Puerto Rico and several other small Caribbean islands became American territories. Guam was taken by the United States. The entirety of the Philippines became American in return for a $20 million payment to the Spanish.

Though he had won an enormous amount from the Spanish, it was not clear that McKinley would be able to get the treaty ratified. There was strong anti-imperialist sentiment in the United States. Buying the Philippines from Spain could not disguise the fact that an American empire was being built. McKinley scheduled the ratification vote for early February to give himself plenty of time to campaign, and set about winning the Senate to his side. In addition, McKinley organized and sent a civilian fact-finding mission to the Philippines to report back how best the United States could resolve the tensions between the two sides. The first Philippine Commission, led by Cornell University president Jacob Gould Schurman, an avowed anti-imperialist, set off for the islands in late January.

It was not clear that the commission would reach the islands in time. In the Philippines, the treaty added to what was already a tense situation. The American and Philippine units had been sitting opposite each other on a line through the outskirts of Manila since the fall of the city. In the south and west, the American line consisted of the old Spanish fortifications, a row of blockhouses and entrenchments. In the southern suburbs, the line ran along the Concordia Creek and the Pasig and San Juan Rivers. Near where it left the San Juan River, the line was cut by a pipe that led from the city to its water supply, a reservoir controlled by the insurgents. Finally, as the line pushed northwest toward the beach, the American defenses fell behind the Spanish blockhouses, crossed over the Manila and Dagupan Railway, the capital city's major land connection to the rest of the archipelago, and reached the shore. Along the entire line, roughly 15,000 American troops faced about 13,000 Filipino troops. Both sides had fortified themselves by digging trenches and putting up earthworks.

Realities on the Ground

Each side eyed the other warily. The relationship, shaky to start with, had been poisoned by the events of August 13. The Filipinos felt betrayed by the American refusal to allow them into Manila. General Merritt's handling of the situation contributed to the problems. The day after Manila capitulated he had issued a communiqué to the Philippine people, laying out American policy. It was a brusque, authoritative document that, for all appearances, assumed uncontested U.S. control of the islands. By August 18 Theodore Wurm was hearing from his regimental comrades that "the Insurgents were acting ugly."[51]

Merritt was smart enough to appoint a liaison between the Americans and insurgents, Maj. J. Franklin Bell. Bell spent much of the following months negotiating with the insurgent commanders. Through Bell, a rough modus vivendi was arranged. The insurgents agreed to turn the pumping station at the reservoir back on so that the city would have fresh water, and Merritt agreed to a number of insurgent demands, including permission for insurgent officers to enter Manila carrying their sidearms.

This uneasy truce might have paved the way for a cordial denouement had not McKinley intervened. Wanting someone with expertise in the Philippines to accompany the American negotiating team in Paris, McKinley ordered General Merritt to France and replaced him with his second in command, Gen. Elwell Otis. Otis, trained at Harvard Law School, had a legal mind, though he had spent almost all of his life afterward in the army. We have already seen his view of the insurgents. Putting him in charge of the situation was not quite throwing a match in a pool of gasoline. It was close, though.

Otis started things off badly in early September by issuing a lengthy letter to Aguinaldo laying out the transgressions and offenses of the insurgents since the occupation of Manila and demanding that the Army of Liberation withdraw completely from the Manila area. Aguinaldo agreed to modify the lines, but not to withdraw completely.

In the fall months, the situation grew increasingly tense. There were confrontations between individual soldiers and between Otis and insurgent officers. None of this was helped by the fact that Otis and Dewey were also arguing over policy, most notably over how strongly Dewey should enforce naval control not just in Manila Bay, but in inland waterways like the Pasig River, much of the length of which ran directly between American and insurgent lines. In addition, Aguinaldo's own position was less than completely assured. He was on the one hand arguing with a group in Hong Kong—the so-called Hong Kong Junta—who represented the interests of a large number of wealthy factions, and on the other hand having trouble controlling his own subordinate officers, especially the ones in the Manila area, who were growing increasingly frustrated with the standoff with the U.S. Army.

The close proximity of the American and Filipino soldiers had also caused a great deal of friction over the past six months. As one soldier wrote in December 1898:

> I believe it only a matter of time when there will be a clash, for the two armies' outposts are within a mile or two of each other, and a single shot from either side would precipitate a general engagement.[52]

To this should be added Filipino frustration over not being allowed to occupy Manila, American frustration with the living conditions, a growing belief on the part of many of the volunteer soldiers that—with the end of the Spanish-American War—their term of service was up, and American racial attitudes. Exacerbating these factors was boredom. The surrender of the Spanish garrison had left the American soldiers with little to do for months afterward. The result, that fall, was a turn to anything that would provide entertainment. Cockfighting became popular. Venereal disease rates—a sign of the oldest form of entertainment—jumped. The men drank anything they could find: *beno*, a potent native liquor, was popular, as was the beer served in bars set up by American breweries almost immediately after the fall of Manila. The drinking caused particular problems, as drunken soldiers misbehaved, brawled, and fell prone to using "contumacious and insulting language" to their officers.[53]

The result was a series of confrontations on larger and smaller scales between the two forces. As Ernest Hewson, a soldier with the First California Regiment, remembered in January 1899: "Where these sassy niggers used to greet us daily with a pleasant smile and a Benhos Dias, Amigo, they now pass by with menacing looks, deigning not to notice us at all."[54] Gunfire between the two lines was not infrequent. A number of times, large units of both Filipino and American soldiers were on the brink of attacking each other, as on December 21, when General Anderson assembled four thousand troops to attack Filipino units disputing the position of an American sentry.

Though the incidents were settled short of open conflict, the situation was chaotic and tense when the news of the Treaty of Paris arrived in January 1899. Aguinaldo issued a public pronouncement in reaction to the news. "I hoped that once the Paris conference was at an end my people would obtain the independence promised them. . . . But it did not turn out thus." This, from "a nation which has arrogated itself the title, 'champion of oppressed nations,' " Aguinaldo continued. Surely, he said, "the conscience of mankind may pronounce its infallible verdict as to who are the true oppressors of nations and the tormentors of human kind." Thus, Aguinaldo said, "My government is ready to open hostilities. . . . Upon their heads be all the blood which may be shed."[55]

Despite the harsh words, however, Aguinaldo was not declaring war quite yet. The treaty had not yet been ratified by the U.S. Senate—which would meet again in early February 1899—and Aguinaldo believed that anti-imperialist sentiment in the United States would prevent that ratification. And Aguinaldo had other problems at that point. A local movement in northern Luzon—the Guardia de Honor de Maria, founded by the Dominicans—was becoming more and more resistant to his control, blaming the revolutionaries for the arrest of many of the local friars, Dominican and otherwise. The Guardia began to organize against the insurrectos. In late December 1898, the province of Tarlac, well north of Manila, had broken out into near rebellion. Aguinaldo was forced to move troops from around Manila to deal with the revolt, unsuccessfully; the problems continued into the month of February and after.[56]

But if the news of the treaty did not lead to open fighting, it did dramatically increase tensions on both sides of the line, as the insurgents and soldiers continued to eye each other warily. A sense of inevitable conflict began to seep through both sides; war at least would break the tension of the months of waiting. "Insurgent scares getting to be a chestnut," remembered John Russater of the First North Dakota on January 11.[57] On January 19 Otis wrote to Dewey that "the insurgent army is becoming very tired of doing nothing and demands blood."[58] Two days later he wrote, "I am convinced that the insurgents intend to try their hand in a very short time—how soon I cannot tell."[59]

Otis and the other American officers worried most about

a simultaneous attack from outside the city and an uprising in the streets. This would force the Americans to fight two battles at once, in opposite directions. Their worry was justified. Aguinaldo and his officers had organized military units inside Manila and covertly brought in arms for them with orders to attack should fighting start.

In the end, the decision to start the war was taken out of the hands of both commanders. The break came finally on February 4, 1899. Exactly what happened to start the fighting has long been disputed, but the general outlines are reasonably clear. The area surrounding the pipe that ran from the reservoir into Manila was particularly touchy. The First Nebraska Regiment was positioned there in such a way as to be surrounded on three sides by Philippine forces. Because the Americans lacked sufficient numbers to garrison the entire line, the defense actually consisted of a series of outposts, backed up by central reserve forces. The isolation of each outpost, combined with an insurgent habit of infiltrating in and out of American lines, made the Nebraskans edgy.

On the evening of February 4, a patrol of soldiers from the First Nebraska was moving outside a village that both sides claimed. Near Blockhouse 7, occupied by the Filipinos, the patrol encountered a group of insurgents. The insurgents and later Filipino historians claimed that the American soldiers fired without provocation. The American soldiers and historians believed that the Americans fired after the armed and advancing Filipinos refused an order to halt. What is not in dispute is that shots were fired, the American patrol raced back to its lines, and a general exchange of fire began all along the First Nebraska's front. This fire soon spread to other parts of the line, and quickly both side's forces were engaged in a chaotic fight in the darkness. There was little chance for Otis to control things; most of the organizing was done at the regimental level and below.

Most historians have focused on the question of whether one side or another deliberately started the war to gain an advantage, whether it was Aguinaldo provoking a conflict to cement his control, or McKinley starting something to help with the Senate vote on the ratification of the Treaty of Paris. What historians have tended to ignore, however, is why this overnight incident became the actual start of the war. There had been similar incidents and encounters, some even on a scale resembling that of the night of February 4, although admittedly without exchanges of fire. All of those incidents had been dealt with by negotiation, and a feeling on both sides that war was not wanted. What made February 4 different?

There is one obvious part to the answer. The Treaty of Paris made it clear to both sides that an amicable and mutually agreeable solution to the differences between the Americans and Filipinos was unlikely. After news of the treaty reached the archipelago, the justification for restraint lost much of its force for both sides.

There are other elements, however. Aguinaldo, despite the centralization of military and political power in his own hands, did not tightly control his forces. The Army of Liberation consisted of a variety of units loyal to a variety of factions. Soldiers were often loyal to their officers, who saw themselves as cooperating with rather than subordinating themselves to higher command. And those men and officers were frustrated by months of waiting and a series of apparent setbacks to their cause. Aguinaldo's prestige had also suffered because of his continuing accommodations with Otis. The result, it seems, on February 4, was less a planned assault on American lines than a spontaneous and unorganized attack. The surprise in the higher Filipino command seems to support this interpretation. A planned simultaneous uprising within Manila was not ready, and Aguinaldo himself was away at a social event when the shooting started.

Finally, the American response went some way toward determining the course of events. Brig. Gen. Arthur MacArthur, who commanded the troops north of the city, had, in the months leading up to February 4, laid out a relatively detailed contingency plan. He was particularly concerned with the vulnerability of his defensive lines. In that area the Americans held a line south of the old Spanish fortifications. They were—as everywhere else—thinly spread. MacArthur felt that vulnerability intensely, and decided that in the case of an attack, the best response was not to wait but to launch an immediate counterattack to drive the insurgents back and give the Americans some breathing room. This was a reasonable response to a difficult tactical matter, but it guaranteed that any outbreak of fighting could potentially trigger an American assault. A few months earlier there had been room for hesitation and negotiation, and a chance to draw back from the edge. Now there was none. Both sides expected a war to start, and both sides got what they expected. "Hell has broke loose at last," thought Private William Henry Barrett of the Second Oregon Regiment.[60]

Three

"AT THE CANNON'S MOUTH"

As morning dawned on February 5, both sides gathered themselves after the night's fighting. The combat had been small-unit work, with squads and platoons attacking and counterattacking. Both high commands were short of information and unclear as to exactly what was going on. But now the darkness had cleared, and the two sides were ready to brawl.

There were roughly 13,000 American soldiers under the command of General Otis that morning. About 11,000 of those were in the lines around Manila, while roughly 2,000 were in the city itself. Most of these were volunteers serving in units from the Western states. Despite the fact that, technically, their enlistments were up with the end of the Spanish-American War, these men seemed eager and enthusiastic to fight. Their frustration at the previous six months of inactivity and the perceived arrogance of the insurgents only added fuel to the fire. As one member of the First Nebraska said, shortly before the fighting broke out: "If they would turn the boys loose, there wouldn't be a nigger left in Manila twelve hours after."[1]

The soldiers were organized into two divisions, each with two brigades. Commanding the First Division, with responsibility from the southern beach line to the Pasig River, was Major General Anderson. Anderson's Second Brigade, commanded by Brig. Gen. Samuel Ovenshine, consisted from south to north of the Fourth U.S. Cavalry Regiment (six troops), the First North Dakota Regiment, and the Fourteenth U.S. Infantry Regiment. The First Brigade, commanded by Brig. Gen. Charles King, consisted of the First Wyoming Regiment (one battalion), the First Idaho Regiment, the First Washington Regiment, and the First California Regiment. Commanding the Second Division, with responsibility from the Pasig River to the northern beach line, was Brig. Gen. Arthur MacArthur. MacArthur's units, in order from the bay to the river, were: the First Brigade, commanded by Brig. Gen. H. G. Otis (no relation to Elwell Otis), which consisted of the Twentieth Kansas Regiment, the Third U.S. Artillery Regiment, the First Montana Regiment, and the Tenth Pennsylvania Regiment; and the Second Brigade, commanded by Brig. Gen. Irving Hale, which consisted of the First South Dakota Regiment, the First Colorado Regiment, and the First Nebraska Regiment. Both divisions were backed up by artillery, the First Division by units of the Sixth U.S. Artillery and the Second Division by the Utah Light Artillery.

The morning of the fifth, both commanders asked Otis

for permission to go over to the attack. Otis agreed and both MacArthur and Anderson launched their troops into the assault. The prospect was not, at first, promising. The Filipinos had had many months to fortify their lines and connect the blockhouses with lines of trenches and other emplacements. If they fought tenaciously, they could inflict heavy casualties on the attacking Americans.

The troops in MacArthur's Second Brigade attacked first, at 8:10 a.m. The First Colorado and First Nebraska Regiments struck Blockhouses 5, 6, and 7, and the lines in between. In both cases, the units took their targets relatively easily. The First Nebraska, in fact, made it past Blockhouse 7 and captured the San Juan Bridge and Hill beyond it, putting them across the San Juan River.

To the south, Major General Anderson ordered a general advance against the lines of the Army of Liberation. It met with similar success as had greeted the Coloradans and Nebraskans. Anderson recounted, in his after-action report, the assault by seven companies of the First Wyoming and First California:

> The movement began at 8:20 A.M. with a rush over the creek on our front, a cheer, and rattling volleys as the whole line advanced, not by rushes, but with a rush. The insurgent line fell back before our advance, fighting, however, with spirit. The rice-fields in our front were intersected with little irrigating dykes, and behind each of these, a stand was attempted, the Filipinos firing from behind them. Our men disdained these shelters and moved steadily on until raking fire was opened on them from the redoubt in the neck of the bend between Pandacan and Santa Ana. The Idaho Regiment made a turn

to the left, charging the redoubt, carrying it at the point
of the bayonet, and driving a regiment of insurgents to
the bank of the river.²

It is here that we begin to see what would become a common theme in the six months of conventional war between
the Army of Liberation and U.S. forces in the islands. The
Philippine forces found it enormously difficult to hold any
positions against a determined American attack. Even, as
noted here, when the fortifications were as strong as six
months of building could make them, U.S. units could
usually storm them successfully, and with relatively light casualties. Even frontal assaults against a "redoubt" capable of
"raking fire" proved successful and usually much more
costly to the Philippine forces than the American.

Why?

The question is why? American troops—especially the volunteers—did not have extensive training. They had little recent fighting experience, with most limited to the Manila
walkover as their introduction to combat. The Army of
Liberation, on the other hand, had a fair bit of experience,
having spent most of 1898 capturing large chunks of the
archipelago from the Spanish. They were on their home
ground, supposedly fighting to defend their people and
their government. Theodore Wurm, for one, was reasonably
impressed with the military capability of the Filipinos. As
he wrote, after nearly a month of fighting:

It must not be supposed that these people are an un-
trained mob, for such is not the case. They can deliver a

perfect volley by company, and understand taking advantage of any shelter which is offered.[3]

But his estimation is not borne out by what happened on the ground. The point is not only that the Americans defeated the Army of Liberation, it is that the defeat was so completely lopsided. American casualties during the first few days of fighting—fifty-nine dead and three hundred wounded—were minuscule compared to Filipino, which numbered in the thousands. This ratio is odd enough, but doubly so for an attacking force. Compare American casualties on February 5, 1899, in which nearly the entire Eighth Corps was involved, with the casualties of the one serious fight between the Americans and the Spanish in Cuba on July 31, 1898. There a Spanish assault on the American lines south of Manila was repulsed by the Tenth Pennsylvania and the First California. Losses amongst the Pennsylvania regiment were nine killed and forty wounded; numbers for the California regiment were likely similar. In a much smaller engagement, the Americans, who were on the defensive, experienced roughly 30 percent of the total casualties of February 5. On February 5 the Tenth Pennsylvania suffered one dead and six wounded, substantially less than in the July attack.[4]

Compare this also with the American campaign in Cuba during the Spanish-American War. The major battle, for the city of Santiago during early July 1898, witnessed the same sort of frontal assault by American troops against prepared positions as occurred at Manila. The number of American troops engaged was about the same as at Manila, but the number of enemy troops at Santiago was much smaller, about 1,700. Despite that, American casualties in Cuba numbered 210 dead, with 1,180 wounded. Why? "To carry earthworks on foot . . . when these earthworks are held by unbroken infantry armed with the best modern rifles, is a serious task," explained the former assistant secretary of the navy and then Rough Rider, Theodore Roosevelt.[5]

There seem to be a number of explanations for the poor showing of the Army of Liberation. The effect of naval gunfire should not be underestimated. At both the north and south ends of the American semicircle around Manila, Admiral Dewey's ships pulled up close to the shore and unleashed barrages on Philippine forces. In addition, American gunboats pushed up the Pasig River and brought the weight of gunfire to bear farther inland than the guns in the bay could reach. The effect of large-caliber naval weapons on a land force was devastating. But we should note that even in areas where the naval guns could not reach—such as in the suburbs northwest of Manila—the American advance was still relatively easy.

Another possible factor was a difference in technology. Some of the American soldiers had much better small arms than the Filipinos. The 1898 Krag-Jorgensen rifle was one example. It fired a .45-caliber bullet accurately to about five hundred yards. Though the rifles the Filipinos were armed with, mostly German Mausers, supposedly had the same range, Philippine ammunition was inferior and often homemade, with all the consequences for accuracy that such a fact implies. And even that ammunition was in short supply. As early as September 1898, commanders were pleading with Aguinaldo for more ammunition:

> We have no Mauser cartridges; I hear there are many in
> Batangas. Americans pay a good price for empty car-

tridges and shells. I ask your excellency to order General Noriel to send us shells; the General has a factory at Paranaque. I am sorry for our soldiers. I see that the more they work and the more they expose their lives, the less they receive.[6]

The limited amount of ammunition meant that the Filipinos had little opportunity to train with live ammunition. In addition, many of the insurgents did not even have rifles and were forced to rely on native weapons like bolos. Finally, although the insurgents did have a number of light artillery pieces and a few machine guns, they do not seem to have had anything that matched some of the heavier American artillery.[7]

But that is not quite enough. The Krag-Jorgensen had its own problems. The war came shortly after its introduction, when the army was having to deal with the rifle's teething pains. Munitions factories were having great difficulty producing consistent ammunition with the new smokeless powder, various rifle ranges could not be used because the Krag-Jorgensen's field of fire outranged their safety limits, and army rifle doctrine had not been rewritten to reflect the new technology.[8] Worse, the Krag-Jorgensen's magazine had to be reloaded cartridge by cartridge instead of by multi-round clip, as the Mauser used. The difference was enough that the army replaced the Krag-Jorgensen almost immediately after the war with a new model, the 1903 Springfield, which relied on a mechanism similar to the Mauser's.[9]

Second, many of the American soldiers, especially those in the volunteer units, did not have the Krag-Jorgensen rifle, but the old Springfield, a single-shot rifle that used black powder. It was slow to fire, inaccurate, and, worse, emitted a great cloud of smoke when fired, fatally marking the firer's position. The soldiers of the First North Dakota, for example, all had Springfields during February and March. On March 31 each company of the First North Dakota received twelve Krag-Jorgensens, enough to outfit the scouts and designated sharpshooters. The rest continued on with the Springfields. The tactical effect of this could be profound. Frank White, a lieutenant in the First North Dakota, forbade his men to fire at insurgents from their prepared position so as not to disclose its location: "I have ordered our men not to do any firing unless we are attacked and so we do not shoot at individuals or squads of soldiers passing along our front."[10] In essence, the range difference meant that the Americans had to attack constantly simply to get into range of the insurrecto trenches.

Further, the insurgents had had similar problems and worse when fighting against the Spanish, and had nonetheless been impressively successful against them. Clearly, the lack of ammunition and the sparse training had an influence, but it seems unlikely that it could have caused such a disparity in casualties.

What, then? Let me suggest that another factor was the client-patron relationship that still dominated Filipino society. The Army of Liberation was, in essence, a collection of patrons along with their clients, the ordinary soldiers. Aguinaldo's control over them was limited, but more importantly, there were certain distinct limitations to how much each patron could demand of each client. For many, death was not one of those demands. The result, in many instances of combat, was that the insurgents would fight fiercely for a certain amount of time, and then make individual retreats when they felt that they had done their duty by their patron.

Further, the duties demanded of the client were best done in a visible public way that the patron had to lead or, at least, acknowledge. During the period between August 1898 and February 1899, the insurgents staged a number of public displays that seemed designed to demonstrate their loyalty and dedication. Sgt. Charles Mabry, of the Utah Light Artillery, remembered one such event, though his account is filtered through his own preconceptions:

> One insurgent officer was particularly abusive. He would gather a crowd of drunken natives, and they would march down to the bridge for the purpose of harassing and scoffing at us. They were encouraged by the apparently submissive attitude of the Americans, whom they had begun to look upon as cowards.[11]

There is a sense here of demonstration that, despite Mabry's evaluation, was more calculated to satisfy Filipino needs than to intimidate the Americans. On the fateful February 5, a Sunday, many of the officers were absent from their units visiting family. The result was that units were left without leadership—fatal enough for any military—but also that clients were left without patrons for whom to demonstrate.

This is certainly not true of all the insurgents; thousands fought and died on February 5, trying to hold the Americans back. But thousands did not, and the limited resistance they offered allowed American soldiers to get in and around the Philippine lines with minimal casualties. When the Tenth Pennsylvania attacked up the road to Caloocan on February 5, the insurgents followed exactly that pattern, as the Tenth's commander remembered:

> Cheering and yelling, the Pennsylvania soldiers advanced rapidly, the enemy replying with heavy volley firing, until the men of the Tenth Regiment were within three hundred yards of the hostile position. Then the insurgents broke and made a precipitate retreat.[12]

In essence, the Filipinos fulfilled their obligations by firing volleys at the Americans until the risk became unacceptable and then retreated. Such behavior had two critical effects on the defense. If the insurgents retreated when the Americans closed within three hundred yards, then most of their fire was likely from much farther than that, well beyond accurate range. At that range, with homemade ammunition and a general lack of live-fire training, one would expect that the defensive fire would miss by going over the heads of the Americans (troops unused to the heavy recoil of rifles would let the barrel rise as the bullet fired, sending the projectile high in the air).

That is, in fact, exactly what the commander of the Tenth reported.

> Their [the Filipinos'] fire had been high and wild and the regiment's casualties were one man shot through the right lung and one slightly wounded in the right hand.[13]

None of this is to suggest that the Filipinos were cowards or were being cowardly. The thousands who died fighting on February 5 testify to that. It is, however, to suggest that many Filipinos, officers and men alike, had a different cultural conception of what war meant and how far to take the fighting. Combined with difficulties of logistics and training, and coming up against a Western army unified by a potent nationalist ideology, such cultural preconceptions created serious difficulties for the Army of Liberation.

By contrast, American soldiers seem to have come from a life that prepared them well for service in the military. Many of them were country boys with extensive experience with firearms. Many could, as Herbert Reddy bragged upon enlisting, "hit a squirrel in the eye at thirty paces."[14]

These cultural differences came together on February 5. Throughout the day, American offensives continually overwhelmed the defenses of the Army of Liberation and pushed American lines outward. Inside the city the story was similar. Otis had been long worried about a simultaneous offensive by the Army of Liberation and an uprising in Manila proper. That is, in fact, exactly what Aguinaldo was planning. The clearest evidence for the fact that the events of February 4 took the Filipinos by surprise is that there was no real and concerted assault within the city limits. Instead, as news of the fighting in the suburbs spread, there was a sporadic and disorganized series of attacks in various parts of Manila. But the army commanders were prepared. As soon as news of the fighting on the outskirts poured in, Otis ordered the Provost Guard to take to the streets and impose martial law. This they did. The Second Oregon and Thirteenth Minnesota Regiments patrolled Manila and skirmished with the insurgents they found. There was a certain amount of fighting and a large amount of arson, but the insurgents never came close to disrupting American control of the city. As the lines outside the city expanded,

some of the Provost Guard was pushed out to occupy critical areas, most particularly the area around the reservoir
and waterworks.

Thus, by the time evening came, the U.S. Army had won
a substantial victory inside and outside the city at little cost
to itself. The Filipinos, on the other hand, had suffered a
substantial defeat and thousands of casualties. Conventional war had begun, and so far all the advantages lay with
the United States.

The War Continues

Manila was safe. General Otis spent the next few days stabi-
lizing his line and reorganizing his troops. The unexpected
success of the attack had caused the Americans some problems. For example, they could not find the First California
Regiment. As Otis recalled later:

> Colonel Smith, with his Californians, had not halted at
> San Pedro Macati, but had pursued the fleeing enemy
> up the Pasig River. No one seemed to know definitely
> [their] location, except that it was somewhere in the
> vicinity of the town of Pasig, Pateros, or Taguig.[15]

In addition, there were a fairly large number of Filipino soldiers caught behind the lines as the Americans advanced,
and many of them turned to "bushwhacking," sniping, or
other attacks. Otis detailed troops to clear them out.[16]

As soon as Otis had organized the mopping up, he
turned his attention to a renewed offensive. The first prior-
ity was securing Manila's connections to the rest of the
Philippines. Its sea-based communications were, of course,

assured by Dewey's ships, but there was a critical land-based connection: the Manila and Dagupan Railway, which rode the shoreline of Manila Bay up to the marshaling yards at Caloocan, a few miles north of the city.

The marshaling yards gave access to the great inner plains of Luzon. Capturing the railway yard there would secure Manila's position for the foreseeable future, and it would allow the American forces to push forward toward the most economically important areas of Luzon. Further, it would bring the Americans closer to the insurgent government in Malolos, and force Aguinaldo to consider his own safety. Caloocan was the bottleneck; if the insurgents could hold it, they could potentially corral the Americans in the Manila area.

At least for a moment; given the absolute naval superiority the United States possessed, there was little hope of holding them to Manila forever. But holding Caloocan would be a start. And they did not have to hold it for that long. The summer rainy season started in June and essentially made sustained campaigning impossible for several months. If the insurgents could hold for that long, the weather would relieve them, and give them time to plan, rebuild, or negotiate.

It is worth looking at the geography of Luzon before discussing MacArthur's campaign. The southern half of the main part of the island consisted of flat plains bracketed on either side by mountain ranges. The great bay at Manila pushed into that plain and left a narrow corridor between the southern province of the Batangas and the rest of Luzon, a corridor further pinched by the Laguna de Bay. Directly to the east of Manila was the Sierra Madre mountain ranges, which extended from the Batangas all the way to the northern tip of Luzon at Escarpada Point. North of Manila ran the railway and the open plains halfway up the island to the regional capital at Dagupan on the Lingayen Gulf.

The military implications of this in the spring of 1899 were fairly obvious to everyone. I have already discussed the situation with Malolos and Caloocan. The American goal—as both Otis and MacArthur recognized—had to be to disperse the insurgent army in the area around Manila, take control of the spit of land that connected Cavite to the Batangas in the south, and ensure that the route to the north was open for further campaigning in the fall. Otis could not hope to end the war before the rainy season; he had neither the time nor the soldiers. But he could create a solid starting point for the campaign that would end the war. Reinforcements were on their way from the United States that would triple and quadruple the size of his command. Starting from Malolos, those reinforcements could conceivably sweep through the rest of Luzon before 1899 ended, and resolve the war as quickly as the campaign in Cuba. But first MacArthur had to take Caloocan.

MacArthur moved forward on February 10 with the Second Division of the Eighth Corps. At Caloocan were about four thousand Filipino soldiers under the command of Gen. Antonio Luna, perhaps Aguinaldo's most trusted military subordinate. As they moved, John F. Bass, the correspondent for *Harper's Weekly*, watched:

> From La Loma church you may get the full view of our long line crossing the open field, even, steadily, irresistibly, like an inrolling wave on the beach. Watch the regiments go forward, and form under fire, and move on

and on, and you will exclaim, "Magnificent," and you will gulp a little and feel proud without exactly knowing why. Then gradually, the power of that line will force itself upon you, and you will feel that you must follow, that wherever that line goes you must go also.[17]

MacArthur planned carefully, and used all the resources at his disposal. After conferring with Dewey, he had the admiral bring up a number of ships to provide fire support. In addition, he located some of his own artillery close to La Loma Church and used that to pound the insurgents. From the left wing, under the guns of the fleet, MacArthur had the Twentieth Kansas and the First Montana advance in a line that started north and then wheeled east, putting the soldiers' backs to the ocean. As the insurgents responded to that threat, the Tenth Pennsylvania, positioned to the right of Blockhouse 2, overlooking Caloocan, opened up flanking fire upon the Filipinos. Some of Luna's forces stood and fought vigorously; others refused to go into battle or retreated without orders. The result, by the end of the day, was that Americans had taken the town and, most critically, the railyards.

Luna had an interesting reaction to the failure. He began gathering troops for a counterattack, but he also began imploring Aguinaldo to reform the Army of Liberation. Luna's ideas, which developed over the next several weeks, were to create a military academy to train Filipino officers, to recruit more of the experienced men from the 1896 revolution, and to impose draconian discipline on the ordinary soldiers. He seems to have recognized some of the fundamental deficiencies of the Army of Liberation, and hoped to set about correcting them as quickly as possible.

The question in that mid-February week was whether he could convince Aguinaldo, and whether the Americans would give them the time needed to re-create their army on the fly. The omens were not promising. By the end of the week, Filipino dead for the Manila campaign numbered around three thousand, while American deaths were between two hundred and three hundred. The Army of Liberation had been summarily and efficiently evicted from its lines around Manila. Filipino morale was shaky; many of the government workers in Malolos had abandoned their desks and fled to the countryside in anticipation of an American assault on the capital city. The Americans were positioning themselves in a way that allowed both easy defense and a return to offensive operations whenever necessary. They still controlled little of the Philippines itself, but no one—not the Spanish and not the Filipinos—had been able to slow down, let alone stop, the American assault.

And, though the rainy season was coming on, Otis was not done. The next jump after Caloocan was a target as valuable politically as Caloocan was geographically: Malolos, the home of Aguinaldo's government. The city was about ten miles up the railroad along the coastline, near the northern edge of Manila Bay. Here were Aguinaldo and his councilors and the main structure of the Philippine Republic. Taking Malolos before the rainy season would not materially improve the American strategic or tactical position but it would make a substantial political statement. The news of battles and casualties could be rewritten or censored. The sight of a government fleeing its capital city could not, and it would put an exclamation point on what was turning into a thoroughgoing rout by the Americans.

Otis was not immediately in position to move on Malolos. He had sent the Tennessee Regiment to occupy the port city of Iloilo after its abandonment by the insurgents, and, though he was expecting reinforcements from the United States at any moment, he did not feel that he could risk thinning his defensive line around Manila to undertake a further offensive. This proved a sensible decision, as the insurgents made a series of efforts to break through the American lines in late February and early March. The most threatening of these occurred on February 22, when a force of about one thousand insurgents infiltrated through MacArthur's line in the north (there were swampy areas that were hard to cover) into the Manila suburb of Tondo. That night, the force set numerous fires in the suburb and tried to start a general uprising. American forces came up from the south and pushed the insurgents northward into MacArthur's troops, now alerted. Filipino losses were roughly five hundred, 50 percent of the force, while American losses were slight.

After the twenty-second, the Filipinos continued to attempt to build up forces outside the American perimeter, but they had great difficulties in getting much more than regimental-sized units into place. The Americans, including the First Nebraska, the First Wyoming, and the Oregonians, were aggressive about protecting themselves. Upon spotting the gathering of a Filipino force opposite their positions, they would undertake spoiling attacks to break up the insurgent forces with almost universally the same success as they had had on February 5.

As this was going on, the two sides were also building up their forces. General Luna had begun the construction of fortifications between Caloocan and Malolos and the gathering of troops and ammunition in the city and in the town

of Calumpit, to the north of Malolos. But his task was
made more difficult by an increasing number of desertions
from the Army of Liberation. Perhaps worse, they were
throwing away or selling their weapons, whose scarcity
made them as valuable as the soldiers. Aguinaldo was forced
to issue a decree on March 12, threatening that "any private
in the Army who shall willfully damage the gun or ammunition which he has in his charge, or who shall abandon,
throw away, or sell the same, shall be punished with the
penalty of death."[18]

Meanwhile, there were several important arrivals from
the United States. First, on March 4, were the members of
the first Philippine Commission. Having traveled by way of
Japan and Hong Kong (where one commissioner, Dean C.
Worcester, had interviewed Filipino junta members, while
the leader of the commission, Jacob Schurman, went on a
shopping trip to Shanghai), the commissioners came ashore
knowing that their original mission—to ease frictions between the Americans and the Filipinos—had evaporated.
Nonetheless, they settled in and began to interview a range
of people: army, navy, and Filipino. Dewey they found con-
genial. Otis they found abrupt.

The other important arrival from the United States in
early March was reinforcements. American troops started
arriving on transports from the United States, including
the Fourth and Seventeenth U.S. Infantry, commanded by
Maj. Gen. Henry Lawton. Lawton relieved Brig. Gen. Anderson, who had been promoted to Major General and
posted back to the United States. These new forces allowed
Otis to build up an assault force for a drive on Malolos.
He launched two columns northward, each a brigade,
on March 24. MacArthur commanded the overall assault,

which though slowed by terrain and fighting, made steady progress northward. The terrain, MacArthur reported,

> was found to be in every respect quite equal to the worst anticipations. The density of the jungle, which prevented seeing any distance, made it impossible to keep the troops together, and thereby embarrassed, impeded, and at times entirely interrupted their movement.[19]

Luna's forces dropped back in front of MacArthur, defending every practical line and burning the villages that they had to leave behind.

The encounters resembled closely the ones around Manila. The Americans would come upon a Filipino defensive line and storm it, forcing the insurgents back. For example, on March 27, the South Dakota Regiment came upon a Filipino line in woods just south of the Marilao River. The South Dakota advance guard, bolstered by their reserve, pushed the Filipinos out of the woods, "forcing them back across the river into a strong line of entrenchments on north bank, from which they again routed them, wading the stream waist deep and capturing the entrenchments," as General Hale put it.[20] As before, the Army of Liberation could slow the Americans, but they could not stop them. Even more critically, they could not inflict heavy casualties on them.

MacArthur expected "desperate resistance" from the Filipinos at Malolos. It was the capital city of the Philippine Republic, MacArthur wrote, and thus "a battle was a political necessity." The first reports he received seemed to confirm that idea. American scouts described "formidable fieldworks, well filled with men."[21] But, much to his surprise, when his forces entered Malolos on March 31, they did so "with little opposition and very small loss."[22] Many of the defensive lines were found abandoned and were occupied without a fight, and even in the city itself, the Americans were subject mostly to sniping. The provincial government had fled and the Army of Liberation's units had fallen back on Calumpit, deciding to make a stand there.

MacArthur took stock of the situation. Casualties had been light, numbering 56 killed and 478 wounded in nearly a month of campaigning. As a result, MacArthur thought to push further north. Though the original plan had been for him to stop at Malolos, now that he looked at the geography, MacArthur wanted to take Calumpit. He telegraphed Otis back in Manila: "Calumpit is . . . a strategic point of importance which, in my opinion, should be secured at once as the natural limit of the first stage of the campaign."[23] Otis refused permission for the advance the next day, which was likely a good decision. MacArthur's forces—though combat casualties had been light—had nonetheless been worn down by the long march and disease, and he was low on supplies. MacArthur turned to restocking and rebuilding his troops, and was finally able, after three weeks, to persuade Otis to let him resume his attack. He did so on April 24.

By now, American officers had learned tactical lessons from the first months of fighting. Aggression paid off: the insurgents fired high, their bullets hitting behind the American front lines, making it safer to be up front rather than behind. Most units of the Army of Liberation would crumble if the assault was carried home with vigor. Some officers had learned the lessons very early on. Gen. Charles King, commanding the First Brigade in the defense of Manila, used that knowledge to great effect, as one of his soldiers remembered:

> Until time to charge or do rush work, or things like that, [General King] would make us all lie down or go behind a tree or a stone, while he himself would walk daintily along the line, a target for the whole fire of the enemy, because of his conspicuous uniform, and because he was the only one of us in sight. He was all the time talking to us . . . "Lie down, [expletive deleted in original] it, my boy! Do you want to get your head shot off? Be careful there; don't expose yourself too much, man! Do you want to get what little sense you have shot out of you?" and such talk, with the expletives in just the right places and all the time the bullets whistling around him. . . . you should hear him order a charge; yes, and see him lead it, too.

"That man will never see America again," said another soldier, but King in fact lived until 1933.[24] It is no imputation on his courage to suggest that King had a solid idea that the risk to him was rather less than he made out to his soldiers. It was not an unreasonable ploy, and it was not unusual, either. From here on, it is remarkable how many times American units carried out assaults against prepared positions and at a numerical disadvantage, and yet triumphed. What would have been suicidal against a resilient enemy was just good sense against the Army of Liberation.

This is nowhere more in evidence than in the battle to take Calumpit. General Luna had stationed his main line of defenses just north of the town itself, on the far side of the Rio Grande: four thousand infantry in entrenchments centered on the railway line. The American forces reached the town on April 25 and occupied Calumpit. At the Rio Grande, the Twentieth Kansas and the First Montana edged up to the riverside and traded volleys with the Filipino defenders on the other side. The next morning, Col. Frederick Funston, the commander of the Kansas regiment, took forty-five men half a mile south to a potential crossing point in the river. Under fire, the men managed to get across and launch a flanking assault against the Filipino lines. As they brought enfilading fire to bear, supplemented by volleys from the Americans across the river, the Filipino lines simply crumbled and insurgents began streaming north. American dominance was complete, and there could be little doubt about the future outcome of any battle. Pvt. Walter Combs of the Fifty-first Iowa Volunteers summarized the American battle tactics at Calumpit in a letter to his parents on May 2, 1899:

> The new method of fighting this war is to fire a few rounds—then advance toward the enemy—firing as we go. Using this tactic, the Filipinos cannot shoot at us without exposing themselves—which they seldom do—and they soon leave in a hurry.[25]

Until the Filipinos could hold a position, they had little hope of defeating the Americans in a conventional war.

The Ratification Fight

Back in the United States, news of the outbreak of war reached a Washington, D.C., locked in argument over the ratification of the Treaty of Paris. McKinley needed a two-thirds vote in the Senate—fifty-six "ayes"—for ratification. Early reports in January 1899 indicated that he was short of votes. This anti-imperialist sentiment in the United States came largely, though not entirely, from elite groups in the East. They consisted mostly of Republicans, and were, in essence, the first generation of that party, who remembered the founding of the party in the 1850s and believed that the spirit of liberation and emancipation of that founding was being betrayed by McKinley's base annexation of the Philippines.

As George Frisbie Hoar, Republican of Massachusetts, put it:

> You have no right at the cannon's mouth to impose on an unwilling people your Declaration of Independence and your Constitution and your notions of freedom and notions of what is good.[26]

Some opponents—such as Sen. Donelson Caffery, a Democrat from Louisiana—argued that taking the Philippines would create a commercial and economic problem for the United States, as cheap goods and materials from the islands flooded into the American market and undercut American industries. Some argued against acquiring a foreign colony when domestic concerns were still pressing, and domestic groups still ill-treated. As Booker T. Washington put it: "Until our nation has settled the Negro and Indian problems, I do not believe that we have a right to assume more social problems."[27]

But while the anti-imperialists had loud voices, those in

the GOP had relatively little influence.[28] Their natural allies were across the aisle, in the Democratic Party. This presented a serious difficulty, because the Democrats were split between the adherents of William Jennings Bryan and Grover Cleveland. While both men opposed imperialism, their supporters found it difficult to get along. Adding in Republican anti-imperialists only heightened the political chaos.

The anti-imperialists could not hope to command a majority, but it was possible that they could defeat ratification and thus either force a renegotiation or, more likely, force McKinley into the same constitutional shenanigans that had marked the annexation of Hawaii. But though they fought with vigor, the anti-imperialists were hamstrung from the beginning by disorganization and by William Jennings Bryan's quixotic announcement, in an interview on December 13, 1898, that he favored approving the treaty and then settling the issue of the Philippines afterward.[29]

While the anti-imperialists were riven by dissension, the pro-treaty side put forward a remarkably effective set of arguments. Those arguments included simple political posturing, as when Henry Cabot Lodge argued that the anti-imperialists were, in reality, anti-American:

> To the Americans and their government, I am ready to intrust my life, my liberty, my honor and, what is far dearer to me than anything personal to myself, the life and liberty of my children and my children's children. If I am ready thus to trust my children to the government which the American public create and sustain, am I to shrink from intrusting to that same people the fate and fortune of the Philippine Islands?[30]

Needless to say, neither the Filipinos nor Lodge's children or children's children were asked about his choice.

But the imperialists also deployed a range of more substantial points. They argued that the United States had long practiced a policy of imperialism against Native Americans, and that many of the anti-imperialist senators and certainly the vast majority of the American people felt that this was and had been a wholly acceptable policy. As Sen. Albert Beveridge put it:

> You, who say the Declaration [of Independence] applies to all men, how dare you deny its application to the American Indian? And if you deny it to the Indian at home, how dare you grant it to the Malay abroad?[31]

In fact, the treatment of Native Americans gave the American legal system a set of case law that could be applied to the Philippines. The legal status of Native American tribes within the U.S. legal system, that of "domestic dependent nations," had been established by a Supreme Court decision of 1831: *Cherokee Nation* v. *Georgia*. The ruling as written by Chief Justice John Marshall essentially denied Native Americans American citizenship and made them wards of the federal government, dependent on the goodwill of government officials. By the 1880s that status had been further reduced, as Congress asserted its control more tightly over the reservations. The Supreme Court declared in *United States* v. *Kagama* (1885) that the tribes were only "local dependent communities," rather than nations. This was, in essence, the creation of a colonial people, notwithstanding that it was within the bounds of the United States. On this legal basis, coupled with the decision of the Supreme Court in *Ross* v. *United States* (1892) that the protection of the Constitution did not extend beyond the borders of the United States, the government could essentially rule the Philippines as it saw fit. The United States would not have to bring democracy or citizenship to peoples of a different race if the nation did not feel like it.[32]

The debate raged so much that a British poet took a hand, not that Rudyard Kipling was ever shy about voicing his opinion. In the February issue of *McClure's Magazine*, Kipling published his famous poem "The White Man's Burden," subtitled "The United States and the Philippines." Kipling opened with an unsubtle declaration of imperialist purpose:

> *Take up the White Man's burden—*
> *Send forth the best ye breed—*
> *Go, bind your sons to exile*
> *To serve your captives' need;*
> *To wait, in heavy harness,*
> *On fluttered folk and wild—*
> *Your new-caught sullen peoples,*
> *Half devil and half child.*

For Kipling, as for the imperialists, the Philippines were to be something of a sacred trust, which the United States would watch kindly over. The Filipinos could not be counted on to govern themselves. A benevolent protectorate over the islands would civilize the inhabitants until they were capable of guiding their own fate. Theodore Roosevelt thought it "poor poetry, but good sense."[33]

If the United States did not take the Philippines, the imperialists asked, then who would? No one thought that an independent Philippines would be able to remain so in the face of the avaricious imperialism of the European nations. German behavior in Manila Bay had made everyone aware of that. Nor was the prospect of going back to the Spanish to renegotiate the treaty a pleasant one. As Sen. Henry Cabot Lodge said during the ratification fight:

> The President cannot be sent across the Atlantic, in the person of commissioners, hat in hand, to say to Spain with baited breath: "I am here in obedience to the mandate of a minority of one-third of the Senate to tell you that we have been too victorious, and that you have yielded too much, and that I am very sorry that I took the Philippines from you."[34]

By the beginning of February, McKinley was close to having enough votes. In addition to his reasoned arguments, the president added a substantial dose of pork. As one observer noted:

> If an honest vote could be taken I doubt whether there is a bare majority for the treaty; but all the railroad influence . . . all the commercial interests and every other interests which can be reached are bringing pressure on Senators in the most shameful manner.[35]

But it was finally the news of the fighting in the Philippines that took McKinley over the top. A vote against annexing the islands after February 4 was a vote against the troops. McKinley was to summarize that feeling shortly after the ratification vote in a speech in Boston:

It was not a good time for the liberator to submit important questions concerning liberty and government to the liberated while they are engaged in shooting down their rescuers.[36]

On February 6, 1899, the Senate voted 57–27 to ratify the Treaty of Paris and officially annex the Philippines. Voting for the treaty were forty-three Republicans, seven Democrats, and seven from smaller parties (Populist, Silver). Voting against were twenty-two Democrats, two Republicans, and three from smaller parties. McKinley had held the Republicans together and pulled over enough Democrats to get the treaty ratified.

The victory solidified McKinley's political position. He had managed to win a political battle that, combined with the military victory in the Spanish-American War, made him a popular president, both in Washington and across the land. One of the few things McKinley had to fear was an extended military campaign in the Philippines causing popular unrest at home, and, since the results of the first few days of fighting had been an unequivocal and overwhelming American victory, there seemed little chance of that.

But McKinley was in a somewhat pensive mood the evening of February 6. The potential weightiness of that situation came home to him. The president, Charles Dawes reported, was "much troubled" by the news of the outbreak of fighting, and how the conjunction of the fighting and the ratification "seemed to emphasize the thought of the enormous responsibilities now resting upon him and his country."[37] McKinley bestirred himself enough the next day to send a telegram to Otis, congratulating him on the military victory, but left the general to his own devices as to what was to follow. How should the United States govern this new territory, McKinley wondered, a territory with millions of inhabitants, without a common language or culture, who were unlikely to welcome American rule?

Reaction in America and the Philippines

The victory at Manila was a needed tonic for the U.S. Army at home. Although American ground forces had been utterly triumphant in Cuba, the rampant disorganization, disease, and downright squalor that had dogged army units, both in the staging depot at Tampa and on the ground in Cuba, had brought with it a storm of criticism. Compared to the glittering and seemingly costless victories of the navy, the army seemed an old-fashioned and organizationally senile remnant of a preindustrial age. As one paper put it in early 1899: " 'If we wish Manilas on land, we must equip our regiments as skillfully as we do our battleships.' "[38] The navy was modern—a machine-oriented service that subordinated the individual to the giant engines, turrets, and guns of Dewey's battleships. The army was hopelessly antique, made up of poor Northern city boys, emigrants, and the dregs of American society. The report of the Dodge Commission, created in the fall of 1898 to examine the military shortcomings of the Cuba effort, was released in February 1899, and its critical conclusions reinforced the negative image of the army.

But the soldiers at Manila changed that image. The U.S. Volunteer units that did much of the fighting were almost entirely from the West. They seemed enthusiastic and cheerful and hearkened back to a beautifully rural image of the American frontier, a frontier now believed to be closed but remembered fondly. They fought against inhabitants seemingly much like the Native Americans. The Filipinos were Indians all over again—living on the land, but not using it properly, fascinating in their own right as "harmless and simple children of nature" but doomed to be "forever blotted out by the encroachment" of civilization.[39]

As they had in the West, Americans would civilize the people and the land, enclose it, and cultivate it. American efforts in the Philippines were simply a continuation of efforts on the North American continent, and Filipinos, like Indians, would have to accept that fact. Newspapers expanded "manifest destiny" to include the archipelago. They rhapsodized about the retired soldiers settling in the Philippines and exploiting its agricultural and mineral resources. *National Geographic* spoke of the United States as "fit representatives of humanity, invincible in war yet generous to fallen foes, subjugators of lower nature, and conquerors of the powers of primal darkness." The job of the nation, the magazine continued, was to pick up, not the "White Man's Burden," but the " 'Strong Man's Burden,' " by raising the weak to "enlightenment." The words echoed spiritual, modernist, and Darwinist themes in fascinating combination.

As the campaign continued and American successes piled up, the army gained further respect at home. The successes of February played a large part in getting Congress to agree to McKinley's request for expansion of the army. On March 2, 1899, Congress approved a bill that would maintain the Regular Army at the strength of 65,000 reached in the Spanish-American War and add a further 35,000 volunteers to supplement the regulars. With the National Guard and volunteer units in the Philippines already well over their enlistment time, it would be this force that was to fight the war in the Philippines.

On a popular level, the successes in the Philippines connected to ordinary Americans more intimately than had the previous generation's victories in the Indian Wars. The National Guard and U.S. Volunteer personnel were essentially civilians, temporary soldiers enlisted to fight Spain. Unlike most of the regulars, then, they were well connected to family and friends back home. Their victories resonated quickly at the local level. The Tenth Pennsylvania returned from the Philippines in August 1899. On their way home, they stopped at Yokohama, Japan, where they had the opportunity to play a baseball game against the Yokohama Cricket and Athletic Association, winning 15–5. They were greeted at the Presidio in San Francisco by a delegation of prominent Pennsylvanians who had traveled across the country to escort them home.[40] George Marshall, later one of the most important military figures of World War II and after, but then a young man in Pennsylvania, remembered the return of Company C of that regiment to his hometown:

> [They received a] tumultuous welcome. . . . When their train brought them to Uniontown from Pittsburgh, where every regiment had been received by the President, every whistle and church bell in town blew and rang for five minutes in a pandemonium of local pride. [The parade that followed] was a grand American small-town demonstration of pride in its young men and of wholesome enthusiasm over their achievements.[41]

The war, at least in 1899, was a popular one. It spurred an interest in the larger world, as people sought to understand these strange new lands. Membership in the National Geographic Society would rise a hundredfold over the next decade and a half.[42]

For the Filipinos, on the other hand, the Battle of Manila and the campaigns after were disasters both strange and familiar. Familiar in that the American victory, unless reversed, seemed to promise the same sort of imperial overlordship that the Philippines had experienced in the centuries of Spanish rule. Familiar because the Americans promised enlightenment and civilization, words that echoed the calls of the Catholic church to salvation and grace, if updated for a modern world. Familiar because, though the Americans spoke of their "mild sway of justice" instead of the "arbitrary rule" of Spain, it was hard for the Filipinos to sense a difference.[43] External domination was external domination. The disaster was strange because the Filipinos had had a substantially uninterrupted string of military successes. They had, since the middle of 1898, essentially broken Spanish control over a large part of the islands. They had fought and won a series of battles with Spanish forces to do this, and while they had experienced casualties, there was nothing to compare to the dead and wounded of February 1899.

In essence, then, the Battle of Manila and the campaigns immediately afterward were shocks to the system of the Army of Liberation, shocks from which it needed to recover. Antonio Luna's suggestions were a good start, but Aguinaldo's situation was both hindered and aided by the structure of the revolution. Aguinaldo and the resistance leaders had to keep the Filipinos fighting. That meant getting the elites (the ilustrados and *principales*) and the peasants reasonably unified against the United States.[44] This was both easier and more difficult than it might have seemed: more difficult because the religious, cultural, and linguistic diversity of the islands meant that Aguinaldo had to unify not one people but many; easier because that diversity meant that disunity could not spread easily. A breakdown of fighting spirit among the Tagalog populations of Luzon would not likely impact the Moros of the southern islands. In a sense, the fundamental differences between the Filipinos acted as a cultural firebreak between them, for good and ill. The results of Manila would likely not have much influence on southern islanders, like the Moros, with one exception: Aguinaldo himself.

Much of Aguinaldo's influence was the informal influence that went along with his success. That influence had been growing as the Spanish crumbled. Manila was a setback. Malolos was worse, because it made clear Filipino defeats. On February 7, Aguinaldo had published an account of the Battle of Manila calculated for its propaganda value:

> The treachery of the American Army, which was certain of victory, received its deserved punishment from our brave soldiers who, without losing their serenity for a moment and without considering their inferiority in number repulsed heroically the heavy and treasonable attack. . . . the number of American dead amounts to more than 500. . . . Our loss was much smaller, not exceeding 47 killed and wounded.[45]

The Army of Liberation might know different, but few others outside of Manila. When Caloocan was captured, a similar account appeared in the *Heraldo Filipino*.

The American traitors received another very hard lesson.
They sustained a loss of more than one thousand in
Caloocan. . . . On our side, very small loss. . . . Panic
reigns in the American army, many of the soldiers of
which refuse to fight any longer.[46]

Those reading the newspaper article might have been forgiven for wondering how these harsh lessons learned by the
Americans kept happening deeper and deeper in Filipino
territory. That suspicion was confirmed by the loss at Malolos. No newspaper article could cover up the dissolution of
the Republic's government. The forced retreat from the
capital made it all too obvious who was winning and who
was losing.

There was another problem with rebuilding the Army of
Liberation after Manila. Such a project required the dy-
namism of energetic leaders at every level of the force. Luna
was such a leader, but Aguinaldo, as a result, was jealous of
Luna. Worse, his subordinates were jealous of their positions. Anyone who threatened those, even if it was in the
interest of reform, was certain to run into trouble. Given
this, it should be no shock to find out that Luna himself—
aided by his own brusqueness—became drastically unpopular as soon as he began pushing his reforms, unpopular with
the people around him and, growingly, with Aguinaldo
himself.

Immediately after the battle, however, Aguinaldo turned
to rebuilding the army. He issued a proclamation on February 7 to begin the process. The document is fascinating as a
mirror to Aguinaldo's problems. He first downplayed the
setbacks: "Commanders . . . must cheer up the spirits of the
troops, who have become discouraged on account of a few

small advantages obtained by the Americans through surprises." Then he turned to practical matters: "demoralized" soldiers would have their weapons taken from them and given to officers. Those officers had to "take an oath not to use [the weapons] for the purposes of robbery, assaults, kidnapping, acts of violence, or other improper acts." In addition, those officers

> shall recognize no other chiefs but the zone commanders or provincial commanders respectively, and shall receive the necessary instructions from the latter. They shall move always in combination with the regular forces of the army.[47]

Clearly, Aguinaldo's control over his army, tentative to begin with, was in severe danger of fracturing completely in the wake of defeat. Perhaps the only thing that kept Aguinaldo from losing military (and perhaps civilian) control was that there simply was no one else with more credibility to take over. Luna, his major military rival, was roundly hated by other Filipino officers, for his reform attempts as well as his sometimes seemingly irrational behavior. And, since he had yet to win a battle, his pronouncements were greeted with some skepticism. Apolinaro Mabini, leader of a faction committed to total independence, was from the same Tagalog group behind Aguinaldo and had little independent sway.

At that point, Aguinaldo was the only credible insurgent leader. But that did not stop him from acting against his rivals. In those early summer months, reeling from the defeats and wandering the towns and cities of Luzon in search of a safe refuge, Aguinaldo focused on cementing his position. It may have been less important whom he acted against than that he acted against someone, and Antonio Luna was the chosen target.

In early June, Luna was invited to meet with Aguinaldo at San Isidro, where the government of the republic had washed up. But upon Luna's arrival, he found the president absent and only the presidential bodyguards present. They and Luna cordially detested each other, as Luna had attempted to have the unit disbanded at an earlier date. Exactly what happened next is not clear, but somehow Luna and his aide de camp ended up dead. The claim afterward was that Luna grew angry and abusive. The findings of the Filipino military court make for wonderful reading, so tortured is the language needed to explain:

> Therefore, the sentinel and the guards being insulted by the said General [Luna] and also kicked and cuffed by him and even having had revolvers discharged against them, not only by the General but also by his aide Colonel Francisco Roman, and being still much more wrought up over the gross insults and threats of death which both made against the Honorable President [Aguinaldo], who thank God, was absent in the field, the sentinel and other guards made use of their arms to repel the unjust aggression of General Luna and his aide, both of whom were instantly killed.[48]

No one seems to have given much credence to this version of events. The general belief seemed to be that, like Bonifacio, Aguinaldo had had Luna assassinated. The difference was that, unlike Bonifacio, Luna was not well liked and so his death passed without much protest.

Aguinaldo's position was, as a result, as safe as it could be. The question was, what to do next? Preparing the Army of Liberation for another campaign against the Americans was likely an impossible task. Many historians have pointed out the impossibility of resupplying and rebuilding the army so as to make it effective against the United States, and criticized Aguinaldo for not turning to guerrilla war earlier.[49] There is some merit in that criticism, but it should not be overdrawn. Fighting a conventional war against the United States was as much a political decision as a military one. Keeping a force in the field against the Americans asserted the continuing existence and organization of the Philippine Republic as a unitary and legitimate state. Turning to guerrilla war would splinter the army and government, send the leaders into hiding, and abdicate that legitimacy. Armies fought to assert legitimacy; guerrillas fought to deny legitimacy to their opponents. The difference was subtle but profound, and it was an issue that others before Aguinaldo—notably George Washington—had dealt with. It might sound like a highly theoretical question, but there were practical implications: Aguinaldo had to worry that, should he turn to guerrilla war, many of the officers and politicians might make the calculation that their interests were better served allying themselves with the Americans rather than pursuing a seemingly lost cause. Thus Aguinaldo, as had Washington, insisted on continuing the conventional campaign, despite a near-unbroken string of catastrophic defeats.

On the other side of the lines, Otis began to think about how to end the war. The string of American successes had made him—and most of the Americans—believe that a few more weeks or months of campaigning would do it. Otis

launched a few more pushes out from the areas already conquered, but a concerted offensive would have to wait until
fall. The monsoon season was starting, turning what had
been difficult terrain impossible. In addition, the National
Guard and volunteer units were finally being sent home,
well after the technical end of their enlistments. As replace-
ments, Otis was receiving both Regular Army units and
U.S. Volunteers. They would fight the war to its conclusion
in the fall of 1899, or so Otis devoutly hoped.

Four

A NEW ARMY ARRIVES

Recruiting for the new U.S. Volunteer units had gone briskly at home. Many of the men had taken their discharges from their state volunteer regiments and then joined up with a U.S. Volunteer regiment. Wilmer Blackett, a "ranch hand, circus hand, railroad hand" from South Dakota, had served with the First South Dakota on the "'North line' just outside of Manila" in February 1899. He returned home and almost immediately signed up with the Seventeenth U.S. Volunteers on May 15, 1899. He was still only seventeen years old.[1] Blackett's comrades included other veterans of the Battle of Manila, as well as veterans of Cuba: San Juan Hill, El Caney, and the encirclement of Santiago.

But many were newcomers. The flood of stories about

the Far East had fired the imaginations of many young men back in the United States. As John D. LaWall, growing up in upstate New York, recalled it:

> In the summer of 1899, I was greatly impressed by the opportunity of travel, adventure, and experience offered by joining one of the thirty new regiments which were being organized for service in the Philippines. So strongly did the desire to go and see for myself what these islands and their people were like, and to participate in such an unprecedented war, take possession of me, that I determined to enlist.

LaWall coyly remarked in his memoirs of service that before he managed to enlist (in the Twenty-seventh U.S. Volunteer Regiment) he was turned down twice by the army because "apparently I did not possess the physical requirements." He did not say what physical requirements he did not meet, but did offhandedly mention that he was only fifteen years old when he enlisted.[2]

LaWall's memory of basic training reveals that the army had not completely solved all the supply problems from the Spanish-American War. His first night at Camp Meade, Pennsylvania, he had to sleep on bare wood floors because there were no more straw mattresses available. "[T]his does not sound so badly, when you say it quickly, but in reality, it is a very uncomfortable way of enjoying a night's repose." His other privations do not sound particularly horrendous. He remembered sorrowfully having to do without butter, and having to get used to black coffee.[3]

LaWall and his unit crossed the United States by train, subsisting on beans, canned tomatoes, and corned beef. In

Colorado, sympathetic residents brought fresh peaches to the train on its way through. The recruits were greeted warmly in San Francisco, a warmth which lasted until the first payday. The ensuing drinking spree soured the city's residents on the new volunteers, and ended in a number of courts-martial and reductions in rank. LaWall, better behaved, or at least unconvicted, rose to corporal in the aftermath.

After a few weeks, the Twenty-seventh was loaded onto troop transports and shipped to Manila. LaWall, who had never been to sea before, discovered that there was little sympathy for his seasickness. "A favorite question to put to a seasick comrade is, 'Wouldn't you like a piece of fat bacon tied to a string and drawn up and down your throat?' " During the trip they lost a man overboard, a "poor despairing wretch left behind to combat with his puny strength the vast, inexorable, deep, relentless ocean." When they arrived in Manila Bay in late October, the "battered hulks" of the Spanish fleet were still visible. They were issued a hundred rounds of ammunition, loaded on lighters, and motored up the Pasig River, disembarking upstream near a statue of Ferdinand Magellan.[4] They had arrived, part of Otis's new army.

Among the units arriving was the Twenty-fifth Infantry Regiment, an African-American unit that reached the Philippines on July 31, 1899. As they landed, a white onlooker is said to have yelled, "What are you coons doing here?" to which several soldiers replied: "We have come to take up the White Man's Burden."[5] The arrival of the Twenty-fifth Regiment, and shortly thereafter the Twenty-fourth Regiment and the Tenth Cavalry, all African-American units, highlighted a noteworthy political and cultural conundrum that the American presence in the Philippines was causing back home. African-Americans had, since the end of the Civil War, voted overwhelmingly Republican. Even as the Grand Old Party had moved away from the legacy of Abraham Lincoln, Democratic reliance on the Solid South strategy and Jim Crow laws had kept African-Americans in the Republican camp. The 1890s marked the consolidation of the anti-Reconstruction structure of American government and society. America, North and South, had agreed that Jim Crow should reign supreme. "We have made friends with the Southerners," remarked one Northern politician. "They and we are hugging each other. . . . The Negro's day is over. He is out of fashion."[6] African-Americans feared that the actively virulent racism that was to a certain extent confined to the South after the Civil War was, as a result of the Spanish-American War and a growing sense of American self-confidence, spreading to the rest of the country. "Negrophobia" seemed all the rage.[7] The rise of scientific racism, as exemplified by Social Darwinism, and the increasing allegiance of the Republicans to a colonial and imperialist mind-set, combined with Democratic opposition to the annexation of the Philippines, put many African-Americans into a quandary.

African-Americans were particularly concerned with events in Cuba and the Philippines. American imperialism in those nations seemed to echo the race relations at home, and the black press discussed the issue furiously through 1898 and 1899. Why, many African-American observers asked, was the United States so focused on the Philippines, exerting energy that could be better spent at home? "[T]he government [is] acquiescing in the oppression and butchery of a dark race in this country and the enslaving and slaughtering of a dark race in the Philippines," wrote John Mitchell, editor of the African-American newspaper the *Richmond Planet.* "We think it is time to call all missionaries home and have them work on our own people." How could the Philippines allow themselves "to come under the sheltering wing of a country which has repeatedly demonstrated its inability to protect the lives and property of its own citizens a stone's throw from the seat of government?" thundered the *Indianapolis Recorder.* The sense grew in the United States that if foreign natives of darker hues could not be trusted with self-government, but had to be ruled justly but firmly by Americans taking up the "White Man's Burden," then did that not justify similar and even increased restrictions back home? Jim Crow found his justification written in the annals of imperialism.[8]

And events in Cuba and the Philippines seemed to be influencing events at home. The jingoistic fervor, it appeared to many African-Americans, led to a similarly violent fervor in domestic affairs. Racial violence rose after the Spanish-American War. A series of gruesome lynchings, including that of Sam Hose in Georgia, where the son of the lynched man was given his father's severed finger as a warning to leave town, was taken as evidence that white America had forgotten the antipathies of the Civil War and reunited as one racist and imperialist nation. African-Americans had been left behind. "What a spectacle America is exhibiting today," said William Lewis, an African-American politician in Boston. "Columbia stands offering liberty to the Cubans with one hand, cramming liberty down the throats of the Filipinos with the other, but with both feet planted upon the neck of the negro."[9]

Some African-Americans, however, remained steadfastly

supportive of McKinley's policies. The political calculation of such motives was sometimes readily apparent: to support the Filipinos, said Calvin Knox, the editor of the *Indianapolis Freeman*, was "suicidal" for African-Americans. But much of the language echoed the general pro-annexation language of redemption, often with a personal twist. As Gurley Brewer put it in the fall of 1899: "the natives in these faraway islands in the Pacific are now being offered the same boon that was offered the American Negro in 1861. . . . The future that Lincoln offered the Negro is being fulfilled."[10]

The sending of African-American soldiers to the Philippines created the deepest of ambiguities. Soldiering had long been a valuable and valued career path for African-American men cut off from most other economic and career pursuits. The African-American community fought zealously to protect that path, and reacted furiously to slights, perceived and otherwise, on the vigor and valor of African-American soldiers. For example, in April 1899 Theodore Roosevelt, who had been seen as something of an ally up to then, published an article in *Scribner's Magazine* that impugned the actions of black soldiers at San Juan Hill. The outrage among African-Americans over this "malicious slander" was immediate and long-lasting.[11] In the Philippine situation, the War Department was initially reluctant to consider African-American volunteer regiments, especially ones officered by African-Americans. An unnamed department official wrote:

> I doubt whether half-disciplined Negroes, under the command of Negro officers, if brought face to face with their colored Filipino cousins, could be made to fire

upon them or fight them. If the Negro understands the Filipinos are fighting for liberty and independence, ten chances to one they would take sides with them.[12]

African-American leaders, whatever their feelings about the Asian conflict, pushed the government to reconsider this notion. They might not like the war, but it would not be an excuse further to reinforce the second-class status of African-Americans within the military and without. The result was that African-American units were sent to the Philippines and that a few African-Americans were promoted to officer ranks.

Once they were there, however, the African-Americans found disturbing parallels in the relationships between the Filipinos and the white soldiers. It was an easy step for white soldiers, steeped in the nineteenth century's easy racism, to bring patterns of behavior abroad. The word "nigger" soon came to be used freely, and racist attitudes reemerged. What one black private of the Twenty-fourth Regiment called "home treatment" soon began to provoke resentment among the native Filipinos.[13] The difficulties were profound for African-American soldiers; their duty was to fight against an enemy with whom they had some sympathy, and live among a people becoming victims of the same "diabolical race hatred"[14] that African-Americans experienced at home. One African-American infantryman said that

> I feel sorry for [the Filipinos] and all that have come under control of the United States. I don't believe that they will be justly dealt by. The first thing in the morning is the "Nigger" and the last thing at night is the "Nigger."[15]

The Philippine situation, so distant from the fetid viciousness of the Jim Crow South, shined a light on the bizarre complexity of that racism. African-Americans were not the only ones to object to or notice the use of the word "nigger." So too did officers from the old Confederacy, who insisted that the term be used only to describe African-Americans. Identifying the Filipinos as "niggers" would imply that those same Southerners were committing a terrible social error by socializing at all with the locals.[16]

In the summer of 1899, with the war still conventional and the enemy still visible and distinct, such issues mattered less. But should the war turn shadowy and an increasing importance come to be put on civilian-soldier interaction, then the "home treatment" was likely to cause military as well as social problems.

Such "home treatment" was also likely to become a problem as the United States brought more and more of the Philippines under its direct control. But as American forces pushed outward from Manila, they gained territory that had to be organized and supervised. By the summer of 1899, Otis was becoming increasingly concerned with how to administer the conquered areas. The challenges were no longer simply military. Instead, they were military, political, and social.

Renewing the Campaign

By October 1899 the rains had begun to ease a bit, and both Americans and Filipinos could begin to think about renewing the fight. The last campaigns of the spring and the experience of small-scale fighting over the summer had illuminated new threats for the Americans. The terrain was difficult enough, but adding in the wildly varying climate—heat and rain not the least—made the Philippines a geographic nightmare for campaigning. In addition, a range of diseases attacked the American soldiers, including typhus, cholera, smallpox, malaria, and typhoid fever. The casualties from such diseases were often worse than those from combat. The First North Dakota, returning to Manila in May 1899 after the spring campaign, had four men with gunshot wounds, twenty with malaria, and eighteen with dysentery. Disease was less of a problem on campaign than it was when the units were in garrison, but the physical effort of campaigning was much higher. Between the physical strain of campaigning and the diseases, American regiments—even without experiencing significant casualties from enemy action—could melt away in a space of weeks.

There had been some notable American successes over the summer. General MacArthur, using an armored train to supply fire support, pushed his lines up to Angeles, several miles north of Calumpit. In the south the sultan of Sulu signed the Bates Agreement with the United States on August 20, 1899, in which he submitted to U.S. control, in return for his continued status as local ruler and the allowance of slavery within Sulu. Most of the American energies, however, had been turned to building up supplies and ammunition in the north, behind MacArthur's lines, preparatory to a general offensive in the fall that would occupy central Luzon and, Otis hoped, end the war once and for all. Fighting that campaign would be a mix of regulars and U.S. Volunteers, roughly 20,000 strong.

Otis had also started creating another force: native auxiliaries. Recruiting amongst Filipinos in Luzon and elsewhere, Otis began setting up units, both military and police, that consisted of Filipinos officered by Americans. Understanding the culture, language, and terrain, these new forces, Otis hoped, would provide advantages that American army units could not. He kept them close to home at first. The initial unit was a small group of native policemen for the city of Manila. Serving there would allow them to use their cultural knowledge to full advantage while simultaneously freeing up American soldiers for the front lines.

The first Philippine Commission had managed, unfortunately, to reduce itself to an even greater degree of irrelevancy since the outbreak of war. Schurman and his colleagues had misread the situation in the spring months, egged on by midlevel officers who wanted Washington to send more troops, and had written home that Manila was "besieged" and the Americans were in peril of being swept into the sea.[17] A more mistaken analysis would have been difficult to manage. Then things had gone from bad to worse. General Otis, worn by the stresses of campaigning, had erupted in a lengthy rant at one of the commission meetings, laying into the commissioners, Admiral Dewey, and even President McKinley. Dewey was present and had no hesitation in shouting right back at the general. Relations were further poisoned when Schurman had attempted to go around the general's back by cabling McKinley and proposing a ceasefire and armistice with the Filipinos. McKinley's rejection of this idea was leaked to Otis; Schurman reacted to the rebuff by announcing that he would return to the United States in early July. He did so, leaving behind the rest of the commission, and little else.

The U.S. effort had also said goodbye to another one of its leading figures. In June, Admiral Dewey was sent home and replaced by Adm. John C. Watson. This was something of a lucky stroke for Otis. As can be seen from the Philippine Commission meeting, he and Dewey had never gotten along well. Dewey, who so triumphantly started the American involvement in the archipelago, seems to have felt something of a proprietary interest in it, with the result that he was frequently unwilling to show the army the cooperation Otis required. He was a "blue-water" admiral, loaded with the visions of Mahan, of great fleets and great battles. The minutiae of supply, fire support, and "brown-water" gunboats patrolling rivers bored him. Watson, on the other hand, came to the admiral's berth committed to brownwater operations, and after his arrival naval vessels did yeoman work supporting the army.

Perhaps the most important task the navy undertook during the summer and fall of 1899 was a general blockade of the Philippines. It could not prevent all movement, most particularly between the islands, but it could shut the Philippines off from the outside world. Using gunboats, some of which had been purchased from the Spanish, the American fleet effectively prevented the trade and movement of most contraband between the islands and with the larger world. Since contraband included many foodstuffs, the results of this interdiction included widespread shortages of food on many of the Philippine islands and a general economic crisis in the trading areas.

The effect of the blockade on the efforts of the Philippine Republic should not be underestimated. Aguinaldo's great problem was the lack of cohesion among the revolutionary groups, and the isolation created by the U.S. Navy only exacerbated that. Further, it made it enormously difficult for the insurgent forces to get supplies, either from other areas of the Philippines or from outside countries.

And finally, it gave the Americans a lever to use against the wealthy Filipinos, whose riches were, in many cases, created by or founded on trade. The blockade could thus be both a carrot or a stick, punishing those who resisted and rewarding those who did not.

Thus, Otis launched his offensive on October 9 already knowing that the Americans dominated the overall situation. Aguinaldo and his army were essentially confined to Luzon; it was unlikely that they would get support from the other islands, and both armies knew who had shown their military superiority in the spring. Otis believed that victory was inevitable. His attention thus turned to ensuring that the Army of Liberation suffered a heavy enough defeat that they would either be destroyed or so disheartened that they would give up fighting. Otis did not want them to retreat into the highlands of either east or west Luzon and continue the war from there. His "well-determined plan of operation" aimed to cut them off from either refuge and pin them in the lowlands between converging columns of American troops.[18] Lawton would lead a column to the northeast, up the Rio Grande, and then over to the Lingayen Gulf. Wheaton would land at the southwest corner of that same gulf and then, when both were in a position to prevent the escape of Aguinaldo's forces, MacArthur would push up the central railroad line from Angeles to Dagupan. This triple-pronged pincer movement, Otis hoped, would crush the Filipinos.

It was, to say the least, a confident plan. Splitting his army in the face of enemy forces is never high on a list of sensible things for a general to do, in whatever era. But Otis did not believe his enemy capable of taking advantage. He had their measure, he thought. They could not and would not react quickly and aggressively enough, and the Americans would crush them.

Or so Otis hoped. Things turned out differently on the ground. The problem was not so much the Army of Liberation as it was the geography and climate, combined with frequent logistical breakdowns. By leaving the Manila region, the U.S. Army also left the only thing that resembled a truly developed transportation network in the Philippines. Moving into the central plains of Luzon left the Americans dependent on narrow, unpaved roads and paths that frequently crossed ravines and valleys over fragile bridges. If it rained, the roads turned to mud and swallowed up man and beast alike, and it often rained. Off these routes, the terrain was blanketed with either forest or densely planted crops. The only reasonably enduring transportation routes were the railroad or the sea. While Wheaton's troops would move by sea at first, once they were ashore in the Gulf of Lingayen, they would be dependent on road and river. Only MacArthur's column would remain with a reliable method of transportation.

It quickly turned out that this road and river network was incapable of supporting the rapid movement of thousands of soldiers and, most critically, their supplies. The result was an offensive in trouble almost from the start. Lawton's column, pushing north along the Rio Grande, found itself fighting the environment as much as the Filipinos. What were supposed to be roads on the map turned out to be dirt trails, cut by fast-running streams that were often completely unmarked on the charts. The flooded rice paddies of Luzon agriculture presented their own difficulties. Combined with the leftovers of the monsoon season, these hurdles wore down Lawton's soldiers and severely hampered his supply column. Wheels stuck in the mud, mules died of overexertion, wagons slid into rivers and were swept away. By the end of October the leading elements of the offensive, a brigade under Brig. Gen. Samuel Young, had made it to Cabanatuan, perhaps forty miles north of their starting point. The main column, under Lawton, was still stuck back at San Isidro, short of supplies and, in Lawton's case, temper. On the twenty-fifth he sent a message to Manila summarizing his situation: "Everything quiet. Rains over. Roads impassable. River has risen some 8 or 10 feet. Is bank-full. Small streams high and unfordable."[19] At times Lawton's reports crept over into the plaintive. After a bridge collapsed, he gravely informed Manila, "This is no pleasure excursion." Faced with impassable roads, the fuming general wrote that this was "about the worst proposition I ever tackled."[20]

On October 31, however, the Americans got some choice intelligence. A captured Filipino document revealed that Aguinaldo had decided to vacate the insurgent headquarters at Tarlac, retreat eastward into the mountains, and set up shop at the upland town of Bayombong. This was exactly what Otis had been hoping to block. The general faced a dilemma: could the Americans cut off the fleeing Tagalog president? He decided to try. Otis ordered Lawton to send Young's force northward to San José, one of the major passes into the mountains. Meanwhile, Wheaton, whose troops were preparing to land on the Lingayen Gulf coast, would push southeastward and close the door from the north.

Chasing Aguinaldo

Unfortunately for Otis's plan, Wheaton's landing on the shores of the Lingayen Gulf ran into difficulties. The initial landing on November 6 went smoothly. Supported by naval gunfire, Wheaton was able to put his troops ashore at the town of San Fabian and scatter its defenders. But then difficulties in getting supplies ashore and the inopportune interference of a typhoon on November 12 all conspired to prevent Wheaton from marching southward. Further, Wheaton believed that units of the Army of Liberation were gathering near San Fabian. To spread out his forces in a marching column would entail a grave risk, and the general decided against it.

In doing so, Wheaton ignored the lessons of the past year's fighting. It had been constant aggression, both on the tactical and strategic levels, that had won the Americans their successes; constant aggression that had kept the insurrectos on their back feet and inflicted heavy casualties on them, while keeping American casualties light. Wheaton made the safe, traditional military decision, and it is hard to criticize him. But it was not a decision prompted by the events of the war so far.

Contrast Wheaton's caution with the reactions of Lawton and Young. Both, upon getting Otis's orders, felt them entirely too passive. Young, in fact, suggested to Lawton that the general give him permission to take a small force of mixed infantry and cavalry and push north, leaving behind the majority of his supply wagons. It was aggressive and daring, and in some small way an echo of Sherman's abandonment of the railway line to march through Georgia and the Carolinas during the Civil War. Lawton gave permission, and on November 7 Young and the Twenty-second Infantry Battalion, a group of the native Macabebe scouts, and the Cavalry Brigade struck out from Cabanatuan. Their goal was to push as far north as they could, and hopefully capture or kill Aguinaldo in the process. It was a remarkably bold move. Should Young get cut off by the insurrectos, he was "without the possibility of support reaching them immediately," as Lawton put it.[21] Essentially, Young risked being isolated and cut to pieces by a sufficiently aggressive insurgent force. But it was a move in tune with the lessons the Americans had learned: push hard and the enemy would either crumble or, at least, fail to take advantage of your potential vulnerabilities.

Meanwhile, as might be guessed, Emilio Aguinaldo's situation was dire. The renewed conventional war of October had only reinforced to the Americans the complete inferiority of the insurgent army. An attack on the American lines south of Manila in mid-October had failed with heavy casualties, and another attack on MacArthur's forces at Angeles had also been repulsed with catastrophic results. On November 5, MacArthur and his forces left Angeles and began moving northward along the railroad line toward Tarlac. Even had Aguinaldo chosen to stay, there was no real possibility that the insurrectos could have held them back.

Their destination was particularly telling. Bayombong was high in the mountains, difficult to reach except by a few select passes and roads. In moving there, out of the lowlands, Aguinaldo was essentially declaring that it was simply not possible for the army of the Philippine Republic to defend its government and that, instead, the government would have to rely on geography for a measure of safety. He cemented the symbolic import of that decision on November 13 by deciding, as he left central Luzon, that the Filipinos should give up on conventional warfare and instead turn to guerrilla war to fight the Americans. As the War Department report (based on captured documents) summarized it:

> The insurgent forces were incapable of further resistance in the field, and as a consequence it was decided to disband the army, the generals and the men to return to their own provinces, with a view to organizing the people for general resistance by means of guerilla warfare.[22]

It was a sensible decision, given everything that had happened, but it was crushing to Aguinaldo. He had brought the republic to the point of controlling nearly the entire Philippines. He had penned the Spanish into Manila. For just that brief moment, they had tasted the sweetness of victory. Now, it was ashes. Now, it was not even clear that he himself would remain at liberty.

He did, but only just barely. Moving north and east to try and get into the mountain passes and reach Bayombong, Aguinaldo found himself, on November 14, just moments ahead of elements of Young's column, which had dashed quickly north. That night, at the town of Pozorubio, Aguinaldo's mother and son were captured, and the president himself had to make a quick escape northward. "If Young does not catch Aguinaldo, he will at least make him very unhappy," General Lawton wired back to Otis.[23] The general was right; Aguinaldo at this point was deeply unhappy, desperately searching for a getaway route.

He gave up on reaching Bayombong and instead headed northwest, over the southern end of the mountainous

Cordillera Central. Getting across the Cordillera would put him on the coastal road heading into northern Luzon, where he could safely hide in a number of places. Aguinaldo's medical officer, Simeon Villa, kept a diary of their movements and on November 15 wrote of the hardships of crossing the mountains:

> The rain was incessant and there was a great deal of mud. The hard wind and the cold made us shiver. We continued the ascent of the mountain, and, as we had already reached an elevation of 500 meters, it seemed that we were at a great altitude and pretty close to the sky.[24]

The American columns were close behind, and several units coming up to serve as Aguinaldo's rearguard were scattered before they could reach the president. On the nineteenth he dispatched Simeon Villa to go to the coastal town of San Fernando, meet with Gen. Manuel Tinio, and organize a further escort. Villa took his horse and rode to San Fernando. As he was riding, "he [Villa wrote in the third person] did not see an American vessel that was lying off the shore until it fired several cannon shots at him. The shooting continued, the Americans perhaps believing that Villa was a general or colonel because he was on horseback. For fear he would be wounded he dismounted, left his horse, and got in the midst of the *cogon* [a weed] patches." He made it into San Fernando and met with General Tinio, who had also had difficulties reaching the town:

> The two, being utterly worn out through hunger and fatigue, went to sleep. About 3 o'clock they suddenly awoke, startled by the firing of guns inside the town it-

self. As it kept up, they went out into the streets to see what it was. Great was their astonishment on finding that the American cavalry was passing and firing on the town. Tinio and Villa escaped by running away immediately; but they had the misfortune to be seen by the enemy, who pursued them. They went up into the mountains and hid.[25]

It was a cavalry unit, led by General Young. Despite the falling away of most of his command, either to sickness or to the end of their endurance, Young had not given up. He gathered as many healthy cavalry troops as he could find and dashed off to San Fernando. There, the general defeated the insurgent garrison with a few hundred men and the help of a navy gunboat, much to Villa's and Aguinaldo's discomfort.

Young was about out of soldiers and supplies. He was forced to borrow $2,500 from an American tobacco company in San Fernando to buy food for the men he had left. He pleaded with General Wheaton to send reinforcements but Wheaton refused. Young turned to the navy, and managed to get the gunboat *Oregon* to go to Vigan, near the northern end of Luzon, and occupy the city.

That put Americans to the north and south of Aguinaldo along the coast and forced him to turn inland and go through the Tirad Pass and into the mountains. On November 30 Aguinaldo's party arrived in Cervantes, up the pass. Villa, again: "As this town offered good conditions for defense, an abundance of food, and a beautiful view, the honorable President decided to stay there for a long time and defend himself."[26]

There was little Young could do to pursue Aguinaldo. He

simply did not have the men. Here fate intervened. On November 26 a battalion of the Thirty-third "Texas" Regiment, the "Fighting Thirty-third," commanded by Maj. Peyton J. March, caught up with Young. Young immediately sent March and his men to chase Aguinaldo up the Tirad Pass. The battalion, which had seen some sharp fighting at San Jacinto but had not undergone the severely draining marches that Young's command had, raced forward enthusiastically and quickly worked its way into the pass.

In Cervantes, Aguinaldo got the bad news about March's unit on December 1 from the twenty-two-year-old prodigy in command of his rearguard, Gen. Gregorio del Pilar. As Aguinaldo escaped to the east, del Pilar had his force of sixty men build fortifications across the trail through the pass and waited for the Americans. The insurgents held their fire until the Americans were close, and then opened such a barrage that the first two companies were driven to ground. March ordered most of his men to hold their positions and sent another company to flank del Pilar. Flanking, in this case, meant climbing up steep cliffs in order to find their way around the defenders. But the soldiers managed, using whatever came to hand, to make ropes: blankets, belts, straps, and so on. When, after several hours, they had struggled their way around to the side, they opened a withering fire from above on the insurgents at the same time that the rest of the battalion charged. Del Pilar was killed as he looked above the wall to measure the situation, and the Americans overwhelmed the rest of the insurrectos. Only nine out of sixty Filipinos escaped.

March resumed the chase, but Aguinaldo's lead was too great and he could not catch up with the president.

"Aguinaldo," March reported, "has been driven to the mountains, a fugitive without a command."[27] It was there in the mountains that Aguinaldo would hold that desperate meeting described at the beginning of Chapter 1, a meeting that ended with his continued flight for safety and refuge. Sitting there in the darkness Aguinaldo may have felt himself shifting from president to prey. Simeon Villa certainly did: "Corporeal fatigue prostrates us; darkness terrifies us; yet we continue our journey, almost crawling," he wrote on December 21 of climbing a mountain at night.[28] The words could have applied to the whole journey. Aguinaldo fled and the army and government of the Philippine Republic fled along with him.

It had been ten months since the war started, and the Philippine Republic had essentially ceased to exist. American power, military and otherwise, had proven overwhelming. Aguinaldo's fall from grace was the fall of many; they had gone from victors to hunted. The native government could no longer assert sovereignty over the islands with any conviction. Now all that remained to them was to dispute America's claim to rule. Whether they could do that with any conviction, success, or endurance remained to be seen. In December of 1899, the possibility seemed remote.

Five

ONE WAR ENDS, ANOTHER BEGINS

Aguinaldo left behind the Army of Liberation in his escape, and as the news of the government's decision to turn to guerrilla war spread throughout Luzon, the officers and men of the Army of Liberation weighed their choices. They could, as Aguinaldo had, melt into the mountains and continue the fight using irregular tactics. They could return home as individuals and sit out the rest of the conflict. They could surrender to or ally themselves with the Americans.

This was what Aguinaldo had feared about the transition from conventional to guerrilla war. The Philippine Republic was losing, and losing badly. For many Filipinos that meant, quite reasonably, figuring out the best resolution for their own situation.

For example, in northern Luzon, the Cagayen Valley was occupied by a force of about 1,200 men under Gen. Daniel Tirona, a close personal friend of Aguinaldo. In fact, Aguinaldo's original flight to Bayombong was predicated on the assumption that there he would be protected by Tirona's force. But Tirona began to have other ideas, and when the American ships *Newark* and *Helena*, commanded by Commodore Bowman McCalla, showed up at the city of Aparri, on the northern coast of Luzon, Tirona began negotiations. The general eventually agreed to surrender himself and his forces, and McCalla immediately appointed him acting governor of the valley and his officers to lower posts.

McCalla was not even really there to wage war or accept surrenders. A small force of American soldiers from the African-American Twenty-fourth Regiment, under Capt. Joseph Batchelor, had gotten lost in the Cagayen. Batchelor's original orders had simply been to move north and occupy Bayombong. But he quickly reconceived them to direct him to invade and conquer the entire Cagayen Valley. His announcement of this, in a letter back to General Lawton in late November, was greeted with some disbelief. As Lawton put it, "His departure for Aparri was as much of a surprise as though he had started for San Francisco."[1] Nonetheless, Batchelor and his soldiers moved northward. The resulting march was epic; the unit hiked all the way through the Cagayen Valley, fighting as they did so, and made it to within eighty miles of Aparri. Batchelor's aggressiveness was an exaggerated version of the push that had served the American army well so far in the campaign. And like that larger aggressiveness, even Batchelor's overwrought actions did not result in the destruction of his unit. Instead,

McCalla's ships were sent to find him, and a gunboat sent up the Cagayen River from Aparri located the battered unit, worn by constant fighting and marching. Batchelor was not particularly pleased to see the navy, and even less pleased to hear that Tirona had surrendered to McCalla. As McCalla put it in a letter to Young on December 14, 1899:

> Batchelor has done splendidly, but he is very much disappointed that the insurrectos in this province surrendered to me. His actions now tend to produce discord between the army and navy and to set the natives against each other. I therefore suggest that it might be well to order Captain Batchelor to report to me officially, until you can come here yourself.[2]

Tirona's surrender was to foretell the gradual co-optation of many Filipinos by the American forces and the gradual whittling away of Aguinaldo's support. The transition from conventional to guerrilla warfare left each commander, for a moment, his own man, free to make his own decisions. Until formal lines of communication and command could be constructed, Aguinaldo—or whoever was in command—could have great difficulty bringing such commanders to heel.

Tirona had more freedom than most. For the majority of the Army of Liberation, stuck in Luzon with the American forces closing around them, the choice was much more limited and unpleasant. Melting away into the mountains meant abandoning any equipment they could not carry personally, meant leaving the most densely populated areas of the Philippines and heading into the difficult terrain of the mountains, meant becoming, essentially, fugitives.

Nonetheless, thousands of insurrectos tried to slip out of the closing trap, while American units worked to bring them to heel. Both were, to some extent, successful. American forces moving throughout the central Luzon plain captured or killed hundreds of Philippine insurgents and took enormous quantities of their equipment. This was small-scale warfare, as the giant net swept in hundreds of tiny fish.

For a sense of the action, let us look at a particular unit, the Twenty-fifth Regiment, the African-American *soldados negros,* as some Filipinos called them. On November 19, 1899, 400 men from the Twenty-fifth Regiment captured the town of O'Donnell and the insurgent garrison there: 105 men, 273 rifles, and thousands of rounds of ammunition. "No casualties on either side," said the official report, an indication that the garrison most likely surrendered without a fight.[3] This was not always the case; units of the same regiment were attacked on January 5 by an insurgent force estimated at around one thousand men (although that estimate was likely exaggerated). They repulsed the insurrectos without loss. The combat itself was confused, frequently at close quarters, and marked (as always) by confusion and chaos. The American army depended on its small-unit leaders—lieutenants and captains—to wage such war effectively.

It is worth quoting one of those small-unit leaders at length to give a sense of the experience. Lt. William T. Schenck of the Twenty-fifth Regiment wrote of a battle on Mt. Arayat in central Luzon in which he led a scouting detachment. They were scouting a hill on January 6 when unseen insurgents opened up, killing a corporal and wounding several other soldiers. Schenck continued forward:

When we got within forty or fifty feet of the top I saw
one of the insurgents, and he seemed to locate me at the
same time, and let drive, and the bullet went right over
me. I yelled at one of the men on my right to kill the
"hombre," and two of the scouts let drive and missed.
Then I took a rifle away from one of the men and fired.
The bullet struck a root in front of the insurgent and
went through, missing him by not more than six inches.
I thought I had him sure and crept up a little higher.
Then he ran up and I ducked and he landed a bullet between me and Sergeant Lightfoot. A mighty close shave—
worse than the first. I got mad then and dragged out my
pistol, handed back the rifle, and crept up on my stomach under a rock and then raised up and fired a shot at
him. This time I was not thirty feet away. My pistol
missed fire the second time and I dropped back. The
stone protected me and I lay there and looked around to
see how many men there were with me. Martin was on
my left and Lightfoot on my right with three other
men—and that was all we had. So I knew we would
have to get some more there or else we were all gone.

But of course, it was not that simple.

Just then someone in the rear opened up and then the
whole outfit—about seventy men—turned loose. We
poor devils on the hill were right in it then. Three bullets
hit just below my feet, fired by my own men. The insurgent tried another shot at me, which went high—thanks
be to God—and the rock. I curled up like a worm to
make a small target for my men, and yelled like a stuck
pig to cease firing.[4]

Schenck managed to get his soldiers to stop firing, organized his unit, attacked, and carried the hill. He was killed in an ambush a few weeks later, by insurgents rather than his own men, but his account suggests just how chaotic the combat was, and how important it was for the American army to have aggressive and able junior leaders.

Despite the battles and the searching, thousands of insurgents escaped into the mountain ranges, often with nothing more than a rifle and the clothes on their backs, but free for the moment to continue fighting. They were joined by a deserter from the U.S. Army who would gain a bit of fame over the next year. David Fagen, an African-American soldier of the Twenty-fourth Infantry, defected to the insurgents in November 1899 and was given a commission in Aguinaldo's army. In addition to leading units against the Americans, he also penned insulting letters to Gen. Frederick Funston.

Despite Fagen, the war seemed over. "We have the rebel army pretty well wiped out," bragged Pvt. Charles Wafer of the Ninth U.S. Volunteer Infantry from Tarlac on December 7, 1899. "All there is here is rain, piss ants, and mosquitos, and they are as big as junebugs."[5] General Otis certainly thought that the war was nearly done. The campaign, though it had not gone entirely according to plan, had resulted in the defeat and dissolution of the enemy army, a mark of success in any operation. The only conventional stronghold for the Philippine Republic in Luzon was south of Manila, in the Cavite province. There, a Filipino force under Gen. Mariano Trias protected a still-working insurgent government and besieged the few outposts that the Americans had managed to open up around the Laguna de Bay. But this was the product of Otis's focus on

Aguinaldo and the northern army. Now that the north was secure, Otis could turn south. He planned an offensive to begin in early January 1900. His chosen general was Henry Lawton, whom he called back to Manila in early December to begin planning. Unfortunately for Otis, and more unfortunately for Lawton, the general was killed in a small skirmish outside the capital city on December 19. His replacement, Maj. Gen. John Bates, did not arrive in the Philippines until the offensive was about to begin, and so Otis gave the command to Brig. Gen. Theodore Schwan, his chief of staff.

That offensive, which kicked off on January 4, repeated American successes in the south. Two brigades of U.S. Volunteers and regulars swept through the Cavite province and into the Batangas, defeating the insurgent forces arrayed against them and inflicting heavy casualties. Typical was the experience of the U.S. Thirty-ninth Regiment, which in the first week of the campaign fought four major skirmishes with the insurgent forces and killed two hundred insurrectos at the cost of fourteen wounded.[6] The conventional campaign ended as it had always done to this point, with American victory.

There were some worrying portents, however. The insurrectos, scattered by the American assault, refused to go gently. Led by enterprising officers, they began to put into practice the principles of guerrilla warfare. It was a return to the days of 1896, and they found that old habits came back quickly. In the middle of January, Miguel Malvar, an insurgent officer, reconnoitered an American position at San Tomas, a supply hub for the advancing U.S. forces, by attending the cockfight that took place there every evening. The knowledge gained enabled him to mount an ambush on a U.S. mule train on January 18. The Filipinos drove off the American detail guarding the shipment, killing one and wounding five, and captured the pack mules and their supplies. "Pitiable," said one officer witnessing the American soldiers straggle into San Tomas, wounded and beaten.[7]

But for the most part, the campaign went easily, and by early February Schwan could report the southern provinces pacified. The insurgents were no longer capable of organized action, and

> their attempts on all but individuals, mere squads, or inadequately escorted trains are feeble to a degree and are evidently induced by a spirit of bravado rather than by any hope of success. . . . they emerge from their mountain retreats mainly for the purposes of rapine and murder.[8]

Schwan's disparaging opinion of the insurgents' efforts was shared by Otis. The war, both believed, was winding down. By the end of February, the Americans had successfully occupied the great majority of southern Luzon and faced no large and organized opposing forces. Normal life could resume. "All citizens," Schwan said, could "return to their homes and . . . pursue their peaceful avocations, in which they will not be molested."[9]

Out from Luzon

Victory in Luzon meant that Manila could turn to a new, twofold goal. First, Otis aimed to occupy the rest of the Philippines, or at least the major islands. Second, Otis intended to set up an infrastructure of government and control. With the war ending, the United States had to set about ruling. Otis first broke Luzon itself into administrative districts headed by various of his generals. Then he brought troops back to Manila and organized amphibious expeditions to the other islands. Of particular interest—not only to Otis and to the McKinley administration—were the far southern provinces of Luzon, the islands of Samar and Leyte, and the northern provinces of Mindanao.

On these islands grew the best hemp in the world, critical for rope making. Raised by peasant farmers in the interior and sold to merchants, it was shipped out of the port towns of each province to—among other places—the West Coast of the United States. Rope was a critical component of the U.S. agricultural industry, and the administration, especially as 1900 started and thoughts of the upcoming presidential election filled their heads, listened to the complaints of the rope makers. Those rope makers spoke of a "hemp panic" if the ports were not opened and the trade reestablished. This seems to have been more about competitive advantage than an actual shortage—one company, the Plymouth Cordage Company, had laid in a great stock before the war started, and its rivals had not. This might not have made a difference, but most of those competitors were from New York State, Elihu Root's home state, and the secretary of war paid particular attention to their concerns and passed them on to Otis.[10]

Otis listened to Root, and on January 18 he sent an amphibious expedition to capture the hemp provinces. Scrounging together some troop transports, Otis loaded up the Forty-third and Forty-seventh Infantries under Brig. Gen. William A. Kobbé. The expedition first reached Sargosan City at the end of the Bicol Peninsula of Luzon and occupied it without extensive fighting; Kobbé then approached Legaspi, the most important city in the peninsula, on January 23. There he was confronted by around eight hundred insurrectos under Gen. Vito Belarmino. The following battle reinforced all the results of the northern Luzon campaign. The insurgents were in fortifications, waiting for the American assault. Kobbé went ashore with seventy-five soldiers and managed to flank the fortifications under cover of naval gunfire. The result was a rout, with more than fifty insurgents killed, the town taken, and only a few Americans wounded. Kobbé left an occupying force and moved on to the other towns. By the end of February he had occupied most of the important ports of the Leyte and Samar.

Control of the ports gave Otis enormous leverage. Each was reopened to commerce as soon as it was occupied, and American merchants descended on them, eager to buy hemp. A peculiar three-way trade soon developed. The hemp fields were in the interior, which was still controlled by the insurgents. The insurgents would usually tax the money that the farmers received for selling their hemp. In the towns, controlled by the Americans, the merchants would buy the hemp, pay tariffs to the American government, and sell the hemp abroad. It was, oddly, beneficial for everyone. Otis let such an informal arrangement continue because of political pressure from home, but also because doing so tied the elites in the hemp provinces closer and closer to the U.S. government. The hemp trade was moving again, courtesy of the Americans, and the locals began to think that U.S. rule was perhaps not such a bad thing after all. In a microcosm, what happened with the hemp ports happened in many areas throughout the Philippines.

In addition to the economy, the American occupation forces began to work on legal reform. During the spring of 1900, U.S. officials fundamentally revamped the Filipino legal system, replacing the heavily Spanish-influenced laws with ones of their own. The Spanish system was chaotically intricate and frequently corrupt. It had been based on centuries of precedent, royal prerogative, and decrees. The Americans replaced it with a code that topped out at twenty pages and had 110 articles of law. On top of everything was a Philippine Supreme Court, which had ultimate authority. Below that was an entire structure of courts, judges, lawyers, and proceedings. The code adopted wholesale American concepts such as bail, habeas corpus, and search warrants. The change was so revolutionary that the Americans had to lend experts to the Philippine courts to help Filipino lawyers and judges figure out their new laws.[11]

Allied with that legal reform was a reform of the tax system. The Spanish system had been horrendously complex, with layer after layer of taxes built up over the centuries. In addition, it had been heavily tilted in favor of landowners, at the expense of those below them. The American reform simplified the system and reduced the number and amount of taxes that the average Filipino had to pay. Otis avoided instituting a land tax, officially because he wanted to leave that to a civilian government, but likely also because he wanted to avoid angering the landowners whose support was still critical to American control.

Finally, on March 29, 1900, Otis issued General Order 40, which outlined the organization of Filipino municipal governments. These local governments would be elected by property owners from the middle class on up. They would control their own affairs for the most part, un-

der the supervision of a provincial administrator who an-
swered to Manila. As planned, it was a system that, as Otis
put it, showed the "beneficient [sic] intentions of the
United States Government."[12]

The attempted return to normality had its effect, especially in Luzon. Filipinos began to return and rebuild their
towns, villages, and homes, slowly at first, but with increasing energy. John Clifford Brown, a soldier in the Battalion
of Engineers, wrote on April 7, 1900, of the Mariquini Valley outside Manila:

> This valley was fiercely fought over. It is immensely rich
> and populous and much desired by the insurgent army,
> therefore it was burned first by one side then by the
> other. . . . Now what is happening? The population,
> driven no one knew where, is returned and is busy
> building new houses and taking care of hastily-gathered
> rice. Everywhere was noise and business.[13]

Things were peaceful enough that John LaWall, leaving
the hospital in Manila in early 1900, could march the
eighteen miles back to his unit alone with an empty gun,
and not only make it safely but remember that "the natives
were very friendly, offering me water and rice cake whenever I stopped for a rest."[14]

The continuing success of the campaign and the expand-
ing American control over the archipelago allowed Otis, at
least on a personal level, to declare victory and go home.
That spring, he had started asking to be relieved and replaced by Arthur MacArthur. On May 3, 1900, he sent a
telegram to Washington: "conditions here very satisfactory
and improving, although some difficulty in Samar and

Leyte, which have been satisfactorily met."[15] Essentially, Otis thought that "the war in the Philippines is already over . . . there will be no more real fighting."[16] McKinley and the Department of War agreed the next day.

Mission accomplished, Otis believed. All that was left was to mop up the remnants of the Army of Liberation and perhaps hunt down a few brigands in the mountains. Those tasks he could confidently leave to the new commanding officer of the U.S. Army in the Philippines, Brig. Gen. Arthur MacArthur. His last telegram was a confident one: The "war has terminated," Otis wired. "Leading Filipinos express confidence in early pacification of islands . . . leading insurgents surrendering." There was one tiny nugget of bad news in that same telegram. Early reports were coming in of the ambush of an American unit on Samar that had killed nineteen soldiers. But Otis boarded the steamer *Meade* on May 5 confident that the war was won.[17]

A Political Campaign

Such a mission accomplished was good news at home as well. Though his political position was strong, McKinley was beginning to eye the upcoming presidential campaign. Having the conflict in the Philippines ended well before that campaign became serious would, McKinley believed, redound strongly to his benefit. Conveniently for McKinley, the Philippine victory had created, with one exception, no serious rivals. A political threat from the hero of Manila Bay, George Dewey, fizzled when the admiral proved incompetent at politics. Entering the race for president, Dewey made a series of comic-opera gaffes speaking to reporters, so bad that one supporter wrote urging him to "say nothing, nor write anything that can turn away support and your campaign will be irresistible."[18] It was too late. The one serious rival was Theodore Roosevelt, who had returned from Cuba and managed to get himself elected governor of New York. Roosevelt, in reality, was less of a rival than a problem. He was cordially disliked by many of the political powers in the Republican Party—most particularly Thomas Platt, the boss of the New York Republican Party. Platt wanted to sideline Roosevelt somehow, and the death of Vice President Garrett Hobart offered an opportunity. That office—"about as useful as a pitcher of warm spit," as a later vice president would so eloquently put it— would be an excellent place to hide the reform-minded Roosevelt. Roosevelt, by becoming the V.P., would "take the veil," as Platt put it.[19] The problem for Platt was that both Mark Hanna and William McKinley disliked Roosevelt. They searched the country for a more suitable candidate than the Rough Rider, even looking at Roosevelt's old boss at the Department of the Navy, John D. Long. But when the Republican convention opened in June 1900, there was no consensus candidate for the position. The convention would have to choose.

Roosevelt himself was not particularly interested in the vice presidency. Though he had told Henry Cabot Lodge in July 1899 that he would like to be vice president, he did so more because of his self-perceived political vulnerability in New York ("Utterly unstable," he judged his position).[20] But by December of that year, his hold on the governorship had firmed up and the vice presidency did not seem as attractive: "The Vice Presidency is a most honorable office, but for a young man there is not much to do. . . . It seems to me that I had better stay where I am."[21] His mind remained firm through February: "In the Vice Presidency, I could do nothing. I am a comparatively young man and I like to work. I do not like to be a figurehead."[22] The fact that Platt was pushing him for the office, Roosevelt greeted with a certain touching naïveté. Platt liked him personally, Roosevelt thought inaccurately, but was being pressured by the industries Roosevelt had taken on as governor. In any case, Roosevelt was more interested in remaining in New York, or being in the cabinet, or being appointed governor-general of the Philippines. The vice presidency seemed to him to be a trap. But it turned out that for once someone got the better of both Mark Hanna and Theodore Roosevelt. Despite all of Hanna's maneuverings and Roosevelt's reluctance, Thomas Platt and his allies managed to convince the convention that Roosevelt was their man.

The vice presidency was the only issue that really stirred the convention. The renomination of William McKinley was never in doubt. The party platform was scripted well beforehand to emphasize economic growth and well-being. The issue of imperialism was handled relatively easily. The taking of the Philippines was presented as the inevitable result of the war with Spain. The fighting that had broken out in 1899, the resistance of the ungrateful natives, was a conflict that had been won speedily and without much effort. Any remaining fighting in the Philippines would soon fade. The only unscripted part of the convention was the vice presidency, so the delegates focused their ardor on it. Roosevelt, ever willing to play to the crowd, arrived in the hall in Philadelphia in a cowboy hat and strode down the center aisle to approving roars. "An acceptance hat," one observer called it.[23] To Mark Hanna's dismay, he discovered that behind Roosevelt was a potent if odd coalition. Many delegates from the Western states, who remembered Roosevelt's heroism in the Cuban War, fought hard for his nomination. Combined with the leverage of the New York and Pennsylvania machines, the surge in Roosevelt's favor proved irresistible, and he was nominated for the vice presidency on June 21, 1900.

Roosevelt accepted the nomination with reasonable good humor, though his misgivings remained. In public, he put on his best and loudest face. In his acceptance speech, he did not shy away from foreign policy and made it clear how the ticket would use the Philippines in the political contest:

> The [Philippine] insurrection still goes on because the allies in this country of the bloody insurrectionary oligarchy in Luzon have taught their foolish dupes to believe that Democratic success at the polls next November means the abandonment of the islands to the savages.[24]

In private, Roosevelt was a bit more ambivalent about the nomination. "I should be a conceited fool if I was discontented with the nomination when it came in such a fashion. . . . Edith [Roosevelt] is becoming somewhat reconciled."[25] Mark Hanna on the other hand did not take the nomination well. In the convention hall, as Roosevelt was voted in, Hanna turned to a friend and said, "Don't you understand that there is just one life between this crazy man and the Presidency?"[26] It was to prove an eerily prophetic remark.

At their convention in July, the Democrats again nominated William Jennings Bryan to be candidate for president. It was not an inspired choice. Bryan ran on a platform of free silver and anti-imperialism, neither of which excited much in the way of popular passion. The economy was surging, and free silver had faded along with it. Bryan's standing on anti-imperialism was grievously hurt by his support for the ratification of the Treaty of Paris. In any case, most Americans did not see imperialism as a particular sin. As long as the economy remained steady and the Philippines remained relatively quiescent, McKinley's reelection seemed assured.

Less than Victory

Worryingly for the Republicans, only one of these conditions prevailed. The economy, after a brief soft patch in August and September of 1900, continued growing. The fighting in the Philippines, on the other hand, began to take on an ominous new pattern. There were 442 attacks on American forces, costing 130 killed and 322 wounded in the first four months of 1900.[27] These small-scale attacks on American units continued to grow in intensity over the summer, and it did not seem that the new commander of the American effort in the Philippines could stop them.

That commander, Arthur MacArthur, has become famous in American history largely as the father of one of the great generals of the twentieth century, Douglas MacArthur. But Arthur MacArthur was a fine soldier in his own right. A Civil War veteran and a Medal of Honor winner, he had spent the ensuing thirty-plus years in the army, at every level of command. On a personal level, he could be difficult to get along with; like his son later, Arthur MacArthur was firmly convinced of his own rightness in almost every situation. He loved to use flowery language in his dispatches,

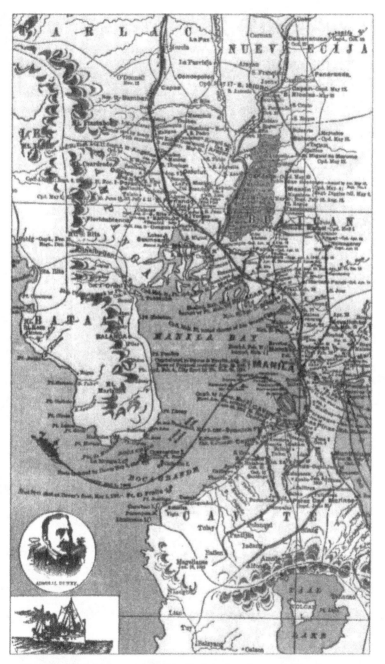

Map of the U.S. Navy attack on Manila Bay, the subsequent American army assault on the city, and the Manila-to-Pagupan Railway line, scene of the American army's breakout from the capital city into central Luzon *(Library of Congress)*

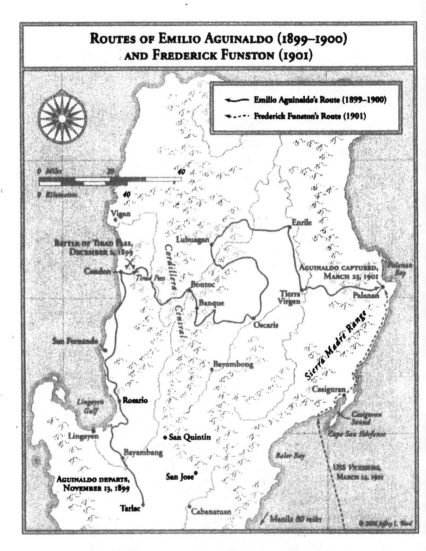

**ROUTES OF EMILIO AGUINALDO (1899–1900)
AND FREDERICK FUNSTON (1901)**

Emilio Aguinaldo's Route (1899–1900)

Frederick Funston's Route (1901)

Vigan

BATTLE OF TIRAD PASS,
DECEMBER 2, 1899

Candon

Tirad Pass

Lubuagan

Bontoc

Banque

Enrile

AGUINALDO CAPTURED,
MARCH 23, 1901

Tierra
Virgen

Palanan

Oscaris

San Fernando

Bayombong

Sierra Madre Range

Casiguran

Lingayen
Gulf

Rosario

Lingayen

Bayambang

San Quintin

AGUINALDO DEPARTS,
NOVEMBER 13, 1899

San Jose

Tarlac

Baler Bay

USS Vicksburg,
MARCH 14, 1901

Cabanatuan

Manila 80 miles

Aguinaldo's desperate wanderings of 1899, and the route taken by Frederick Funston in
capturing the Filipino president in 1901

The wrecked Spanish flagship *Reina Christian* sits in the shallow water of Manila Bay.
(Library of Congress)

A Spanish fort outside of Manila *(Military History Institute)*

Destroyed Spanish munitions after the capture of Manila *(Military History Institute)*

American commanders. Frederick Funston is first on the left, Arthur MacArthur is fifth from the left, and Elwell Otis is sixth from the right. *(Library of Congress)*

American troopship packed with soldiers *(Library of Congress)*

Emilio Aguinaldo
(National Archives)

Emilio Aguinaldo and
son *(Library of Congress)*

American soldiers fire from Blockhouse 13, outside of Manila. Note the waist belts of rifle bullets.
(Library of Congress)

The Twentieth Kansas Volunteers, commanded by Frederick Funston
(Library of Congress)

Frederick Funston *(National Archives)*

The aftermath. Filipino bodies lie on the battlefield. *(Library of Congress)*

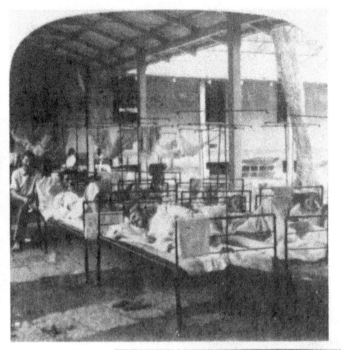

American casualties
recovering in
hospital
(Library of Congress)

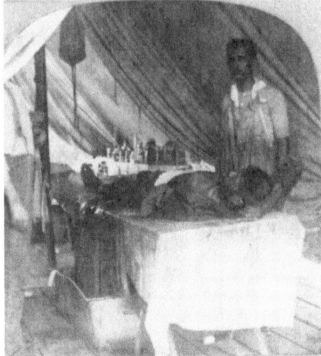

American doctor
operating on a
captured
Filipino
(Library of Congress)

A painting of the Battle of Quingua, April 23, 1899, an early encounter between the Americans and Filipinos *(Library of Congress)*

An American unit fords one of the archipelago's many rivers.
(Library of Congress)

Church at Caloocan,
destroyed during the
American assault
(Library of Congress)

American supplies piled
up at Manila
(Military History Institute)

"Death in the ranks of the Kansans."
(Library of Congress)

Governor Theodore Roosevelt inspects the Twenty-sixth U.S. Volunteer Infantry before they go to the Philippines.
(Military History Institute)

Filipino civilians encounter American soldiers.
(Library of Congress)

Gregorio del Pilar *(National Archives)*

American artillery overlooks one of the U.S. gunships that plied the interior waterways of the Philippines as part of the "brown water fleet." *(Library of Congress)*

Captured Filipino officers in jail
(Library of Congress)

Arthur MacArthur several
years after the war
(Military History Institute)

William Howard Taft, head of the Second Philippine Commission, plays cards.
(Library of Congress)

Simeon Villa captured
(National Archives)

Emilio Aguinaldo,
after his capture,
boards the
Vicksburg.
(National Archives)

and he was not above shading events to burnish his own image.

Unlike Elwell Otis, MacArthur was, from the very beginning, eager to understand how to deal with the situation in the Philippines. As Peyton March remembered,

> [MacArthur] had a standing order with Kelly, the bookseller of Hong Kong, to send to him every book in stock published on Far Eastern matters, particularly those devoted to colonial administration of the various islands and parts of the Far East which were under control of the European powers.[28]

MacArthur quickly recognized what Otis did not; the Filipino revolutionaries had managed to reconstruct themselves organizationally and turn to an unconventional form of warfare that relied on ambush, concealment, and the avoidance of conventional set-piece battles.

Within days of Otis's departure, MacArthur received further news of the attack on Samar that the former commander had glancingly referred to in his last telegram. A unit of the Forty-third Regiment of U.S. Volunteers, thirty-one men strong, had been stationed at the small town of Catubig. There in the middle of April they had been ambushed by a strong force of insurrectos. The ambushers besieged the Americans in the convent that was serving as their quarters and then smoked them out by throwing in burning hemp from the church next door. The Americans attempted to escape downriver, but were cut to pieces as they tried to board their boats. The survivors dug in along the river and held off the attackers until they were saved by a relieving force, but by that time nineteen men had been killed. Was Catubig an isolated incident or the start of a new kind of war in the islands?

Just as such pressing military questions were raising their head, MacArthur's problems became political as well. In early June, members of the second Philippine Commission arrived in the islands, headed by William Howard Taft. Taft, an Ohio politician, a friend of Elihu Root, and a judge on the Sixth U.S. Circuit Court of Appeals, had agreed (somewhat reluctantly) to head the commission and help get a civilian administration up and running. An important question for McKinley and Root was, what should be the relationship between the commission and the military command in the islands? Eventually, the commission would take over governance. With conflict still going on, however, some sort of compromise had to be found. Unfortunately for both Taft and MacArthur, the compromise reached in Washington was ungainly, to say the least. MacArthur would remain both military and civil head of the administration in the Philippines, but the commission would appoint and remove his civil subordinates, pass legislation, and control the financial side. Left unclear was whether MacArthur could veto the legislation, whether the appointing and removal required his approval, and how much budgetary control he had. It was a recipe for friction and ill feelings.

There are various stories about how MacArthur greeted Taft and the other commissioners when they arrived in the Philippines. In some, MacArthur was supposed to have greeted Taft with frigid formality, so much so that the sweat of Taft's brows dried upon his skin.[29] In others, MacArthur was formal, but polite and cooperative, and lunched with

Taft several times in the days after his arrival.[30] In still others, MacArthur went out of his way to arrange an honor guard for the commissioners on their arrival, sent his second in command to greet them, and accommodated, with long suffering, the petty demands that the commissioners made.[31]

However the reception went, Taft and MacArthur soon butted heads. Both sides had a certain amount of justice to their causes. From Taft's perspective, he was there to organize and get the Philippines running now that the war was essentially over. MacArthur's resistance to the presence of the commission was thus simply the stodgy resentment of a soon-to-be superseded military commander. From MacArthur's perspective, the commission consisted of a bunch of overweight civilians (Taft traveled with his own bathtub because normal ones could not contain his ample frame) who had no experience with the Philippines and yet expected him to bow to their orders. Worse, MacArthur's sense that the war was not in fact over continued to grow. Worried that the insurgents were taking the strategic initiative away from the Americans, MacArthur tended to vent his frustration on the commissioners and their assumption of a golden and harmonious peace soon to come.

As part of the process of handing over power to the commission, MacArthur was supposed to declare provinces pacified. He thus followed Otis's practice and kept American forces spread widely throughout the archipelago in garrisons of rarely more than a hundred men and officers, to introduce and enforce American rule. Most of these garrisons were out of direct communication with Manila, and it fell to the commanders of each to explore and understand their localities and figure out how harshly or gently to apply dominion. They would have to serve as the civil and military powers, setting the rules for the ordinary people and chasing down any resistance.

It was MacArthur's only real option, but it carried with it risks. American forces, small in size and distant from one another, were extremely vulnerable if the insurgents ever gathered themselves in large numbers. In addition, the American soldiers were perhaps not the best tools for the job. They frequently understood the Filipinos in explicitly racial terms. When John LaWall described the Filipinos, he instinctively reached for such ideas:

> Imagine an Indian "crossed" with a negro, the product of this union married to a Chinese, and whatever conception you may form of the offspring of such a strange combination should bear an analogy in appearance, if not in mental and moral attributes, to the Filipinos.[32]

These attitudes brought a level of contempt and patronization in the American attitudes toward the Filipinos. Worse, few of them spoke any of the dialects used in the Philippines.

It is clear that MacArthur still hoped against hope that the resistance was merely the leftovers of the Army of Liberation. On June 21, as Theodore Roosevelt was accepting the acclamation of the Republican convention, MacArthur tried a final throw of the dice. He announced a ninety-day amnesty for insurrectos. If they turned themselves in, they would not be punished but only disarmed and sent home. If those resisting were merely stragglers, MacArthur's plan might have been effective. Instead, only a few insurrectos turned themselves in, and the attacks continued.

Guerrilla Warfare

The war that was developing in the summer of 1900 was a less immediately familiar one to the Americans. An American unit, a supply train, or an outpost would be ambushed by a small insurgent force, armed with either bolos or rifles. Pvt. Lewis Cozzens of Company B of the Thirty-third U.S. Volunteer Infantry recalled the incidents during late October and early November. On October 25 the telegraph wires linking the coast to Bangued, the town garrisoned by the Thirty-third, were cut. The American unit responded by sending out patrols to repair the cables. One of these was ambushed by the insurgents, who "greatly outnumbered" the U.S. soldiers. Casualties consisted of six dead and nine wounded. The next day, the insurgents opened fire on Bangued during the night and in the morning ambushed a "raft going downriver to Vigan." On November 1 the insurgents stole an American flag flying outside one of the Thirty-third's outposts, shot five horses, and cut the telegraph line again. On November 2 another company on patrol was ambushed with six wounded. In response, the Americans mounted a surprise raid on a village suspected of harboring insurgents. "The surprise raid was successful," Cozzens reported. "A number of huts were burned, and a large amount of Mauser ammunition was confiscated."[33]

The tactics seemed unfair to the Americans. As John Clifford Brown commented: "The soldier starts with a fine contempt for the insurgent, who would not stand up for a square fight, but who always wanted to fight from ambush and who playfully boloed the stragglers."[34] Soldiers derisively labeled this kind of fighting *amigo* warfare because, after inflicting casualties, the insurgent force would fade away into the jungle, and when the Americans pushed on into the nearest town, all they would find were Filipinos in civilian clothing crying out *"Amigo, amigo!"* as a sign of friendship.

Whenever a village was approached the natives came forward and offered lukewarm water in coconut shells. They were all very profuse in their assertions of good will, smiling all sorts of welcome, but who were at heart insurrectos and who bona-fide partisans of the American invasion it was hard to say. It was simply a case of "Jack-in-the-box." Enter American troops, white blouses, all "Amigos" and smiles; exit Americans, blue print trousers, sullen looks, and "Viva Aguinaldo."[35]

In this war, knowledge was preeminent, but the Americans found intelligence gathering difficult. The American force in the Philippines, said Col. Arthur Wagner, was "a blind giant. The troops were more than able to annihilate, to completely smash anything that could be brought against them . . . but it was almost impossible to get any information in regard to [the insurgents]."[36]

Few of these attacks did much damage or inflicted heavy casualties. Mostly one or two soldiers would be wounded or killed. But there was rarely a chance to strike back effectively, and the American soldiers, used to the conventional fighting of the previous year of the war, found this war of shadows frustrating. What the new kind of war mostly meant for the American soldiers was long stretches of boredom interspersed with exhausting patrols and the occasional bit of action. The war strained the men, as it required them always to be alert, and yet they only rarely encountered an enemy with which to come to grips. " 'While there is no enemy in sight, yet we are always on the lookout and we have slept in our shoes ever since we landed,' " said Lt. J. H. Thomas. "The war may be over or may have just commenced. No one can tell what these devils will do next."[37]

Any distraction was welcomed. Mail from home was immensely popular, and payday was the day of all days. The men spent their pay almost immediately. As one soldier remembered:

> Right then the celebration started. There was one big rush for the dice and monte games, and another big rush for the saloons. I was with the second bunch. I drank everything that the [saloon] sold that night from goo-goo *vino* and Jap *sake* to Schlitz beer and good old Kentucky rye. . . . If the goo-goos had swept down upon the city that night I couldn't have moved a finger to help save the occasion for Uncle Sam.[38]

Neither boredom nor the guerrilla strategy were likely to force the Americans to evacuate, but they did make for good stories in the American media, forced the American army to recognize that it had not been as victorious as it had thought, and convinced many Filipinos that the republic lived. But for victory, Aguinaldo was relying on something else.

Interestingly, Aguinaldo was well tuned in to domestic events in the United States. Despite the fact that he was on the run and frequently deep in the mountains or jungles, he managed to keep up with a range of news stories from America. He often used them against the Americans. In leaflets aimed at African-American soldiers, he went as far as to mention Sam Hose, the African-American from Georgia lynched by a white mob in 1899.[39] And what he read in the newspapers led him to pin his hopes on the U.S. presidential election. If the insurgents could make the Americans bleed a steady trickle of wounded and dead throughout 1900, they could influence the election. Aguinaldo wrote to one of his generals:

> In order to help the cause of Philippine Independence in the coming presidential election in the United States of America which will take place early in September [sic] of this year, it is very necessary that before that day comes, that is to say, during these months of June, July, and August, we should give the Americans some hard fighting.[40]

Aguinaldo's grasp of the date of the election was faulty, but there is some justice in his reading of the campaign that far. Bryan's fiery anti-imperialist rhetoric, filling the media, seemed to dominate the campaign. McKinley faded into the background. If Bryan won, Aguinaldo concluded, he would free the Philippines.

There was an air of desperation about Aguinaldo by the middle of 1900. He was on the run for most of the early part of the year, hunted by Americans and unable to stop in any one place for more than a few days. His personal servant had deserted him one night, taking with him a rifle and a number of rounds. His generals sent him lists of the latest officers to desert the insurrection, and one of the officers of his personal escort had attempted to take his unit and leave Aguinaldo behind. Aguinaldo had him shot, but he could not enforce such discipline on anyone farther away. His rule extended as far as his sight, and sometimes not even that.

Such was the case throughout the Philippines. The revolutionaries not only had to fight the American soldiers but also try to prevent Filipinos from cooperating with the foreigners. They were fighting a two-front war, in essence. On one front they had to keep up their efforts against the U.S. Army; they had to not lose, at least until the presidential election. On the other front they had to ensure that the people of the Philippines, large and small, wealthy and poor, important and obscure, helped them and hindered the Americans. Traitors could not be tolerated:

> Certain residents of the town of Bay, named Domingo Punsalan [and] and Manuel Revilla . . . forgetting they were Filipinos, accepted positions given by the enemy . . . [and] displayed the United States flag in the town hall. The upright and patriotic residents of the above mentioned town, at the sight of such outrageous insolence, invaded the town hall and killed Punsalan and Revilla.[41]

Despite such actions, however, the ongoing American efforts to woo Filipinos to their side continued to have success throughout 1900.

But if the Filipinos were losing on the civilian side, on the military side things were no longer so clearly in favor of the United States. The outbreak of the Boxer Rebellion in China in June had pulled two regiments of American troops away from the Philippines, leaving MacArthur short-handed. The number of attacks on American forces had been going up steadily during the early summer, interrupted only by monsoon season.

The problems made him difficult. Taft wrote back to Root that MacArthur "regards all the people as opposed to the American forces and looks at his task as one of conquering eight millions of recalcitrant, treacherous, and sullen people." Further, Taft complained of "the indisposition of General MacArthur to enter into a discussion . . . or cooperate in any way."[42] It is clear in retrospect that MacArthur's evaluation of the situation was closer to reality than Taft's. It is probably not surprising that the general found it hard to work with the eternally cheerful judge.

After the breathless and soaked interval of the monsoon, things started to slide out of control. The insurgent attacks continued to rise, and the size of the insurgent forces seemed to be increasing. It is sometimes difficult to tell how many insurgents there were. John D. LaWall remembered his unit of sixty men being attacked on September 17, 1900. Their camp, located next to a river, was ambushed at night from across the water. LaWall's account makes it clear that he never actually saw the insurgents. The soldiers lined up on the river's edge and poured volley fire into the "bamboo thicket" across from them, repulsing the attackers, their "occasional shots dying away in the distance as dawn began to let light upon the scene." Despite the confusion of the firefight, LaWall confidently reported that the sixty men of his unit had fought off five hundred insurgents.[43] If such inflated numbers were common, it is no wonder that MacArthur was depressed.

This is not to say that such depression was without reason. Two events, in particular, showed that the war was largely out of American control. In early September, on the island of Marinduque, Filipino insurgents ambushed a force of fifty-six American soldiers of the Twenty-ninth U.S. Volunteers, commanded by Capt. Devereux Shields. After a three-hour firefight, the Americans retreated but were soon surrounded in a rice paddy. Wounded, Captain Shields surrendered himself and his entire command.

Worse was to come. On September 17, a combined force of the Fifteenth and Thirty-seventh Infantry Regiments, which consisted of about 130 men under the command of Capt. David L. Mitchell, came upon a strong insurgent force at Mavitac, in the Laguna Province of Luzon. The insurgents, commanded by Gen. Juan Cailles, had dug in on the other side of an arm of the Laguna de Bay, at the far end of a bridge. The surrounding land was still soaked from the monsoons, making movement extremely difficult. Mitchell did what had served American officers well since the start of the war. He sent his men across the bridge in a frontal assault on the insurgent fortifications. Experience had taught him, as it had taught other American officers, that the insurgents would fire high and would break before the Americans got too close.

Unfortunately for Mitchell's command, the insurrectos refused to cooperate. Instead of firing high, the Filipinos fired accurately. Instead of breaking when the Americans closed to within a few hundred yards, the Filipinos continued to fire. The result was a debacle for the U.S. soldiers and a stunning victory for the Filipinos. Advancing under the heavy and accurate fire, unable effectively to shoot in return at the Filipinos in their entrenchments, the Americans at first pressed the attack and then after an hour broke and retreated. In that hour, twenty-four American soldiers were killed and nineteen were wounded. The Filipinos lost roughly ten dead and twenty wounded. When the American soldiers returned the next day, they found that Cailles had wisely retreated, content to take his victory back with him. MacArthur put the best face possible on the setback in his report. "Thirty-three percent [casualties] is profoundly impressive loss and indicates stubbornness of fight, fearless leadership of officers and splendid response of men." The enemy, MacArthur reported, had no doubt returned home and hidden their weapons "to appear for time being, or until called into fight again, as peaceful amigos."[44]

And that was the crux of it. MacArthur's remarks about "fearless leadership" and "splendid response" were simply a thick coating of whitewash on a profoundly ominous development. The Filipino guerrillas seemed to be developing what the Army of Liberation had never had: the ability to inflict serious damage on an American unit while holding the field of battle. Whereas at Catubig in April, a large force of Filipinos had surprised and trapped a small force of Americans, at Mavitac the two forces had met on the battlefield, neither surprised. The Filipinos had won. If they could do that on a regular basis, and still effectively melt back into a population that would support them with money, food, and other supplies, then MacArthur and the American effort in the Philippines were in serious trouble. The situation was bad enough that MacArthur's son Douglas, then at West Point, would later be heckled at the Army-Navy baseball game with the chant "MacArthur! MacArthur! . . . Who is the boss of this show? Is it you or Emilio Aguinaldo?"[45]

Autumn

The fall campaigning season was thus, from MacArthur's perspective, a particularly critical one. The United States had to ramp up its military efforts and effectiveness. Otis's focus on the civilian side of things had worked to reestablish something approaching normality, and the reforms of the legal and economic systems were clearly successes. But that success was not matched with a similar success on the military front. That quite a few Filipinos were returning to prosperity gave them more resources to spare, and they frequently spared them to aid Aguinaldo's forces. As Capt. John L. Jordan said, "this business of fighting and civilizing and educating at the same time doesn't mix very well."[46] MacArthur's level of stress can be detected in his treatment of Taft and the members of the Philippine Commission. MacArthur's dinner parties conspicuously did not include commission members, and he picked a series of inane arguments with the commissioners, including one in which the general vetoed an appointment decided on by the commission, even though MacArthur himself had recommended the officer.[47]

MacArthur finally decided to turn up the heat on the insurrectos. First, he sent two battalions of soldiers, over 1,200 men, to Marinduque to recover the captured soldiers of the Twenty-ninth U.S. Volunteers, and made it clear to the commander of the battalions, Gen. Luther Hare, that the population was not to be spared: "Regard all the males over the age of 15 as enemies. . . . [They] should be held as hostages until the hostiles are killed or captured."[48]

Second, he formulated a plan to attack the insurgents more aggressively. He would leave most of the garrisons where they were, but pull back a number of troops from more remote or peaceful areas and concentrate them in flying columns of men. These he proposed to send into the areas with the most active insurgents, to patrol aggressively and go after the insurrectos on their own turf.

He laid out the plan for the War Department in a telegram dated October 26 detailing the time frame and the requirements. He thought that "full development" of the plan needed four months, and he "urgently recommend[ed]" that the War Department stop taking troops from the Philippines and sending them home or to China. The next day, the War Department telegraphed back its assent, saying that Root wanted the plan "prosecuted with vigor."[49] As these new troops arrived in the Philippines, MacArthur used them and the surplus troops gained by closing down some of the outposts to build up forces in hotly contested areas. In the northern Luzon province of Ilocos, Gen. Samuel Young saw the troops under his command increase from 3,590 on August 18 to 4,928 on November 3.[50]

Assaults directly on the insurgents were only half the effort required. The Americans had to find a way to persuade the civilian population not to provide the guerrilla forces with money, supplies, or information. The "benevolent assimilation" that McKinley and Otis had promised had worked in some areas and with some groups, but it had not done so in the greater part of the archipelago. Now, MacArthur was determined to apply the whip hand. Marinduque was only the beginning.

The behavior of American soldiers in the Philippines was officially governed by General Orders 100. GO 100 had been written during the Civil War to help Union forces deal with the task of controlling occupied Southern territories.

The author, a distinguished lawyer named Frances Lieber, had had sons fighting on both sides, and he aimed the orders to be stern but fair. "Men who take up arms against one another in public war do not cease on this account to be moral beings, responsible to one another, and to God," he wrote in the orders.[51] He based his guidelines on a range of sources, including the medieval scholar of the laws of war, Hugo Grotius, American policies in the Mexican War, and international laws. GO 100 demanded the fair treatment of enemy soldiers and of civilians in occupied terrain. But it also required that those enemy soldiers and occupied civilians meet certain rules of behavior. Enemy soldiers had to wear uniforms. Occupied civilians could not act to hide or assist enemy soldiers without fear of repercussion.

These rules reveal that Lieber was particularly worried about guerrilla warfare, unsurprising in the context of the Civil War. Guerrillas, Lieber said, were "not public enemies, and therefore, if captured, are not entitled to the privileges of prisoners of war, but shall be treated summarily as highway robbers or pirates." If the civilian population acted to hide or assist such guerrilla forces, the occupying army was justified in punitive destruction of civilian property, as long as that destruction was not "wanton."[52]

GO 100 had been in effect in the Philippines since the arrival of the American army, but Otis had emphasized the gentler side of the order and de-emphasized the harsher. MacArthur had followed his lead, but in the fall of 1900 he began to reconsider that. The punitive measures allowed by GO 100 could certainly be the stick to go along with the benevolent carrot held out so far. Captured insurgents could be executed summarily. Towns giving support to Aguinaldo's forces could be destroyed. The Filipino population could be made to feel the pain of propping up the revolution.

MacArthur hesitated, for political rather than military reasons. The presidential campaign was coming into its last weeks in October. Bryan had been unrelenting in his assaults on America's imperial venture. With imperialism such a critical issue, the War Department did not want to give the anti-imperialists anything that resembled a last-minute issue with which to flog the president, and explicitly turning to harsher methods in the Philippines would be such an issue. Combined with the recent insurgent success, it might tilt the balance against McKinley. MacArthur thus focused first on a renewed military campaign without the harsh new measures while awaiting the election outcome.

The Election and an American Commitment

The Republicans ran a canny campaign in 1900 based on economic good times, promising "Four more years of the Full Dinner Pail." Their vice presidential candidate, Theodore Roosevelt, strode around the country, bellowing loudly from behind his glasses and mustache. He traveled farthest and did his most good in the West, a targeted region for the Republicans. It had voted overwhelmingly for Bryan in 1896 on the foundations of economic depression and the promise of free silver. But now the economy was good, and the Westerners had been enthusiastic imperialists. The Republicans hoped to capitalize. In one Western trip, Roosevelt traveled 12,870 miles and gave speeches to more than 600,000 people.[53] He waved the bloody flag and accused the Democrats who opposed the war in the Philippines of being descendants of the pro-South Civil War copperheads. He emphasized the contradiction at the core of Bryan's platform. How, Roosevelt said, could the Democrats argue for freeing "Malay bandits" when the Democratic strongholds of the Solid South denied "the right of self-government to our fellow-Americans of dusky color?"[54]

That rhetorical device highlighted the contradiction for African-Americans in the election of 1900: neither party seemed attractive. The Republicans had fallen under the sway of imperialism; the racial notions of Social Darwinism drove their views of race relations at home and abroad. Kipling, whose views many African-American Republicans found to be "sham and hypocrisy," was a guiding star for that imperialism.[55] Worse, President McKinley seemed oblivious to African-American concerns, preferring, for example, to condemn the lynchings of five Italian-Americans in his 1900 State of the Union address and ignore the hundreds of lynchings of African-Americans in the same year. Resentment toward Roosevelt still boiled in the African-American community. But the Democrats were no better than the Republicans, captive as they were to their Southern wing, from which so much of Jim Crow flowed. Though some of the Democratic machines of the North—notably Tammany Hall in New York—reached out to the African-Americans, it was not enough. Most of the African-Americans who could vote did as they had done since the end of the Civil War: voted Republican, albeit while perhaps holding their nose.

Creakily, then, the Republican coalition held together on November 2. McKinley won a second term, this time by a larger margin. In 1896 McKinley had garnered 51 percent of the popular vote against Bryan's 48, and 271 electoral votes versus Bryan's 176. McKinley had won with the

Northeast and the Great Lakes states against Bryan's hold on the Solid South and most of the far West. In 1900 McKinley opened up his lead, again taking 51 percent of the vote, but this time to Bryan's 45 percent. The electoral college margin was even wider. McKinley held the Northeast and Great Lakes and shattered Bryan's hold on the West, taking Kansas, South Dakota, Colorado, Utah, and Washington, and losing only Kentucky in return. In a final triumphant slap to Bryan's face, McKinley won the Democrat's home state of Nebraska by a bare 7,000 votes. That gave McKinley 292 electoral votes to Bryan's 155, and a solid grip on the White House. The Republicans also made gains in the congressional elections. What had been a relatively close Republican advantage in the House (187 to 161) became a gaping one. They gained thirteen seats and the Democrats lost ten, making the GOP's majority an unassailable 200 to 151. The Republican majority in the Senate, most of whose members were still chosen by the state legislatures, remained sizable.

The soldiers in the Philippines were split between the two candidates. The officer corps, for the most part, leaned toward McKinley, believing that Bryan and the Democrats would pull out of the Philippines. But the ordinary soldiers seem to have been much more evenly inclined. In a mock election in the Thirty-third U.S. Volunteer Infantry, Company A went for McKinley 23 votes to 13, but Company B went for Bryan 24 votes to 14. The overall count for the entire regiment was 79 for McKinley to 55 for Bryan. The margin was heavily weighed toward McKinley, but, perhaps surprisingly, it was nowhere near unanimous.[56]

In essence, the election of 1900 stood as an affirmation of McKinley's policies, both foreign and domestic. Voters may or may not have consciously meant it that way, but the practical effect was the same. McKinley was confirmed in office, the Republicans were confirmed in their majorities, and thus the policies of the American government were unlikely to change substantially. The United States was in the Philippines to stay.

Reactions to the elections came from both sides of the conflict. For the Filipinos, the election was a disaster. Aguinaldo had pinned his hopes on it, and had made it seem as if Bryan's victory was a foregone conclusion. The news of McKinley's triumph seems to have shattered morale among the insurgents. The concentrated efforts of September and October were now apparently exposed as worthless. From Hong Kong, the head of the junta there wrote on November 10 with the disagreeable news:

> McKinley, our mortal enemy, who aims at our subjugation, whose announced plan is to convert us into servants of his servants. . . . McKinley, we repeat, he who calls us bandits, uneducated and savage, has been re-elected.

The junta "felt this check in the utmost depths of its heart."[57]

The result in November and December 1900 was a wave of surrenders by insurgent forces. At the end of November, over a thousand bolomen came to Santa Maria in northern Luzon to surrender to the American commander, General Young. He did not have the supplies to feed them and asked them to return in a few days. When they did, on December 2, there were over two thousand. "The President's re-election and vigorous prosecution of the war" were the reasons, Young reported to MacArthur.[58] The previous largest surrender that Young had taken was of two hundred insurrectos.[59]

Aguinaldo himself was reduced to wondering if perhaps McKinley might have a change of heart. "Who knows," he wrote on November 12, "but that the Señor [McKinley] may not reestablish our destroyed government. . . . That the great North American Republic with its military honor satisfied and actuated by sentiments of humanity will recognize our lawful rights."[60] These were wistful words from a leader who, two weeks earlier, had written that "it is better to die with honor than to live dishonored and execrated."[61]

On the American side, after the election, American soldiers, officers, and administrators in the Philippines knew that a withdrawal was not imminent. In addition, the cannier among them—and MacArthur should be included—realized that the political pressure had been relaxed, at least for the next year or so. Until the president started thinking about the next midterm elections, the political consequences of actions in the Philippines could be, if not completely ignored, at least downgraded. Thus American forces had to worry much less about the immediate domestic repercussions of their actions in the Philippines.

As a result, MacArthur resumed and ramped up his preparations for a sustained campaign against the insurgents and their civilian supporters. This came with the full support of Elihu Root and the War Department, and surely with that of his own officers and men, who felt that they had been restrained from treating the insurgents and their native supporters with the necessary harshness.

In late December 1900 MacArthur issued two critical communications. The first, on December 20, was to the

people of the Philippines. In it MacArthur laid out the
stringent policy. The harsher provisions of General Order
100 would be strictly enforced. The second came six days
later, when MacArthur cabled Root asking for permission
to deport suspected rebel leaders to Guam. Root cabled
his assent, and MacArthur deported Apolinaro Mabini,
among others, to the mid-Pacific island.

The difficulty with General Orders 100 and with
MacArthur's use of them in the Philippines was that they
left much up to the judgment of the individual on the spot,
whether officer or enlisted man. In the archipelago, where
many units were far distant from Manila, and where lines
of communication stretched for weeks, GO 100 put a great
deal of responsibility on the sergeants, lieutenants, and captains who ran the small garrisons on a day-to-day basis. GO
100 forbade "wanton" destruction, but what constituted
"wanton" destruction? GO 100 allowed for reasonable physical punishment of uncooperative civilians, but what was
reasonable?

Some historians have pointed to the fact that the American soldiers themselves could be harshly punished if they
misbehaved, and that U.S. officers were frequently just as
concerned about the mistreatment of Filipino natives by
their own soldiers as they were about any other form of bad
behavior. American officers, as John Reed has pointed out,
wanted to create the impression of "stern, uncompromising
justice" that applied to soldiers, insurgents, and civilians
alike.[62]

It is nonetheless clear that there were American officers
and men who practiced fairly dubious methods in their
waging of the guerrilla war. Some of these episodes arose
out of lack of knowledge or simple incompetence. John D.

LaWall remembered one of his lieutenants was "such a drunkard that he boasted of his willingness to sell his soul for a drink of whiskey." One night, when the captain of LaWall's company was in Manila, this particular lieutenant was in command. When one of the sentries thought he heard a gunshot, "the drunken Lieutenant had the men fall out, lined them up and ordered them to fire 3000 or 4000 rounds into the sleeping village across the river." A number of civilians were killed, but what was reported was that the "gallant company had routed the enemy."[63]

But some of these practices were official or semiofficial policy. Perhaps the most famous of these was the "water cure." Pvt. Evan Wyatt of the Eighth Infantry U.S. Volunteers recalled how it worked. "Water cure . . . consisted of laying a prisoner on his back and pouring water down his throat until he looked like a pregnant woman." If the initial application did not work, the prisoner would be forced to vomit the water up, sometimes by having a soldier step or jump on his stomach, and the process would be repeated. Wyatt did not enjoy it: "the spectacle was so horrible [that] I walked away."[64]

The water cure has become something of a stand-in for all sorts of physical punishments used to make people talk; its peculiar brutality captured the imagination of observers and historians alike. There is little evidence to suggest that the water cure was more prevalent than simple beatings or mock hangings or other forms of violence. What is clear is that a range of ways was used to get people to talk, and many of them would be (and were) considered forms of torture. Torture was never official American policy, but in many places it became de facto American practice.

MacArthur also took another important step in December 1900. Under a fair amount of prodding from Taft and the members of the Philippine Commission, MacArthur agreed to expand greatly the native constabulary and field forces. Those groups, started under Otis but neglected since, would be used to supplement American troops, to guide U.S. forces in remote areas, to gather intelligence, and to serve as police in various areas, including Manila. The expansion had a number of positive effects for the Americans. It created a force whose members instinctively understood the culture and behavior of those they were fighting because they were usually from the same ethnic group. Native police and soldiers also had access to contacts and intelligence from the community that Americans, hamstrung by their lack of language skills and their racism, could not match. In addition, recruiting men of military age for these bodies and paying them a reasonable wage drained the pool of possible recruits for the insurgents. Finally, having native forces carry some of the burden of policing, scouting, and fighting eased the burden on American forces. For an American commander continually short of men, as MacArthur was, this was a strong incentive. Though it started slowly, the massive increase in these native police and military groups was one of MacArthur's most important contributions to the war effort. MacArthur also encouraged the formation of a Philippine political party, the Federal Party, which supported the American presence in the islands. The leaders of the new party were a range of middle- and upper-class Filipinos, and they stood as a potential political rival to Aguinaldo's Philippine Republic, offering a political refuge for those wavering between the Republic and the United States.

The outline of MacArthur's plan should be clear. He had

put together a military response, deploying garrisons in key areas combined with large mobile forces that would sweep through and seek out guerrilla forces. He had put together a civilian response, targeting those who supported the guerrillas and allowing the destruction of property as a method of punishment. He had put together the beginnings of a long-term response. If the native forces were successful and could be built up, then American forces could be drawn down, critical for any long-term occupation of the islands.

The only thing left to do was to put his plan into operation. Throughout the Philippines, starting in December, columns of American soldiers began to push their way into the mountains and jungles of the Philippines, chasing insurgent bands and struggling through the terrain. The soldiers had had some warning of what was to come: "Companies A and B, Thirty-Third Infantry, were called out to receive new shoes," Lewis Cozzens remembered. "This is always an ominous sign. It usually means that a long march is in the offing."[65]

Mindanao

In the southern island of Mindanao, Brig. Gen. William A. Kobbé and his originally sparse force, now built up through the addition of the Twenty-eighth Infantry, began operations to intensify the pressure on the local guerrillas. "Operations have been continuous night and day since December 8 in all sections, each column, as it comes in to recuperate, finding another ready to take its place."[66]

Kobbé himself led a force of men from the Fortieth Infantry Regiment to chase down a group of guerrillas under the command of Gen. Nicolas Capistrano. Kobbé's aide was Capt. John J. Pershing, who would rise to greater things during World War I and after. Kobbé's force pushed into the jungle in late December in search of Capistrano. As always in the Philippines, the Americans fought the terrain as much as the enemy. "The country was indescribably difficult," Pershing remembered, "mountainous inland, heavily wooded here and there, and cut by rivers and precipitous ravines."[67] The grass rose "to the height of twenty feet . . . its blades are razor like. . . . Frequently the trails are mere tunnels . . . wherein passage is all the way from a stooping posture on all fours to an upright walk, often in mud and water to the waist," remembered another officer.[68] For the infantry, it was bad enough. For the cavalry men and their horses and, more, the artillery unit with its wagons and cannon, it was sheer hell.

But the Americans persisted, and pushed deeper and deeper down the Cagayan River. Capistrano's men harassed them from long range with rifle fire, but refused at first to give battle. Kobbé forced the issue and finally brought Capistrano to ground at a fortified position on December 17. The fort was at the head of a deep gorge, difficult to approach directly. But Kobbé managed to get both men and machine guns on top of one of the gorge walls and they rained fire into the insurgent position. After a two-day battle, Capistrano abandoned the fort and retreated. Kobbé followed. The two fought another battle outside the interior town of Langarang on the twenty-eighth; again the insurgents retreated. Capistrano was too smart to engage in a full-scale battle in which his force might be destroyed, but the continued pursuit by the Americans was having the effect of whittling his forces down anyway, through casualties and desertion.

In addition to his military efforts, Kobbé devoted special care to cultivating relations with the locals. Taking advantage of Mindanao's local feuds and the ham-handedness of some of the Tagalog guerrilla administrators, Kobbé built up his network of informants. Former insurgent officers proved especially useful, giving information on tactics and locations. This is not to say that force was not sometimes used to convince locals to give information, as when Col. William Birkhimer of the Twenty-eighth Regiment, patrolling at Kobbé's orders in northeast Mindanao, sought information on insurgent movements. "Just then we seized a native, who was at the time acting in the double capacity of herder and outpost for the insurrectos and compelled him to show us the way."[69] Birkhimer did not elaborate on how he "compelled" the native. In some cases, the information came from an American. "On December 21, Private Alexander McAlfrey, a deserter from Company I, Fortieth Infantry, came in and surrendered to Captain Green. He gave much information." McAlfrey guided a unit of the Fortieth to an insurgent stronghold that was found to contain "1,800 pounds coffee, 7,000 pounds rice, 7,000 pounds corn," a number of cartridges, and seven brass cannon.[70] The cannon were brought back to the American base; everything else was burned. What happened to McAlfrey is not recorded.

Kobbé also used punitive measures against the civilian population. He seems to have gathered most of the men of military age in the district and confined them in American-controlled camps. American troops also frequently burned towns that were suspected of harboring insurrectos. And units approaching towns do not seem to have been too particular about their initial targets. Upon marching into

the town of Silo, Colonel Birkhimer's men encountered
Filipinos:

> When within about 1200 yards, men were seen moving
> in the town. They discovered us simultaneously. They
> soon recognized us as enemies, ran into the houses
> hastily to get what they most prized and then scattered
> like quail up the mountains. . . . Hastily forming K Com-
> pany in line on a ridge which fortunately offered itself,
> at 1,000 yards several volleys were fired at the disappear-
> ing Filipinos, 5 of whom were found dead in the out-
> skirts of town.

Note that Birkhimer did not have any conclusive evidence
that the men were actually insurrectos. From 1,200 yards, it
would be hard to distinguish them from civilians panicking
at the sight of oncoming troops. Birkhimer, somewhat de-
fensively, immediately after this account, points out that
"there was every evidence that Silo was a rebel cuartel [vil-
lage]."[71] He did not specify what the evidence was.

Kobbé's campaign met with substantial success. By the
beginning of February, Capistrano was negotiating his surrender, which finally took place at the end of March. His
defeat essentially destroyed organized insurrecto resistance
in northern Mindanao. After March 1901, insurrectos remained in the hills, but the network of organized forts,
towns, and supply depots ceased to exist. What remained
was a policing problem, not a military conflict.

$\mathcal{S}ix$

"SATISFACTORY AND ENCOURAGING"

The Mindanao campaign was not an exception. Almost immediately it became clear that MacArthur's campaign was going well. The monthly number of Filipino insurgents surrendering to the Americans rose to over eight hundred in January 1901. Nearly 23,000 small arms were handed in to American forces. MacArthur telegraphed home in the middle of the campaign on January 4, 1901, that "troops throughout the entire archipelago more active than at any time since November '99. Results satisfactory and encouraging."[1]

"Satisfactory and encouraging" continued. And it was not just capturing or killing the guerrillas that made the most difference. Capturing weapons and ammunition was just as critical. The republic was desperately short of both, and rarely able to resupply its forces. It is thus not surprising that General Young in Ilocos was gleeful on January 29 when his men captured an insurgent arsenal that contained thirty pounds of gunpowder, three thousand shells, and 15,000 primers.

The Americans did not have everything their own way, in Ilocos as elsewhere. The insurgents continued to use their tactics of ambush, and now that there were quite a number of American columns out and moving, the ambushers had what might be described as a target-rich environment. Most vulnerable were the resupply trains, moving through the islands to bring goods to both garrisons and mobile forces. On February 2 a pack train of the Fifth Infantry was attacked near Tayum in northern Luzon, with six dead and three wounded. What was different now, however, was what happened next. Pvt. Lewis Cozzens and his unit were detailed to chase the ambushers down. What would previously have been a fool's errand of wandering aimlessly through the jungle now became something quite different. As they moved, local informants kept Cozzens and his unit apprised of the location of the ambushers, and the next day they captured "about two dozen of the enemy . . . who were put aboard rafts and sent downriver to Vigan for interrogation." The impressive immediacy of the capture made it clear that the situation had changed substantially and likely for good. U.S. forces were no longer operating in a vacuum. Now, tracking and locating the enemy were possible and possible quickly.

There is an interesting coda to this story. Cozzens's compatriots were unsatisfied with simply capturing the enemy. Their friends had been slaughtered and they apparently needed more. When they returned to their barracks in

Bangued, Cozzens himself was too tired to do more than collapse into his bunk: "my body was so sore, I could hardly move." But other soldiers of the Fifth Infantry were not: "Twenty men . . . went into town, intending to exact revenge on the local Filipinos." Thankfully, they were stopped before too much damage was done and "thrown in the guardhouse for being drunk and disorderly."[2] The near massacre illustrates the way in which American soldiers tended to lump all Filipinos together.

Ilocos also demonstrated the value of another stratagem, that of starving the guerrillas of their food supplies. Young had made focused efforts to prevent the November rice harvest from making its way into the hands of the insurgents through strict control of the harvest and transportation of the rice, and the forced concentration of the farmers themselves into U.S.-controlled towns. The American effort was magnified in many places in 1900–1901 by an epidemic of rinderpest, a cattle disease that wiped out the domestic stock of the farmers and reduced the rice harvest. The risk of such stringent concentration of the population and control of the food supply was starvation and disease. People rudely pushed together in unfamiliar surroundings, with limited amounts of food, were terribly vulnerable to illness.

It was a winning military strategy, however. Results were showing by early 1901, as major guerrilla bands in Ilocos reported desperate shortages of food. The result was the surrender of over 20,000 guerrillas in the province in the first months of the new year, and the eventual surrender of the heads of the insurgent forces, including the brothers Juan and Blas Villamor on April 29. Manual Tinio, the general appointed to overall command in Ilocos by Aguinaldo, had actually surrendered to Gen. Franklin Bell the day before the Villamor brothers, but when learning of the brothers' capitulation, asked Young to postdate his surrender to May 1. Bell bemusedly complied.[3]

As a reward for the success, Congress promoted MacArthur to major general on February 5, 1901. MacArthur, stuck so long at the rank of captain in the post–Civil War years, had advanced from colonel in under three years. But the success also planted the seeds of MacArthur's supercession. Taft, as it became clear that the insurgency had been, at very least, tamped down, wrote home to Elihu Root, arguing that with normality again returning it was time for the Philippines to be run by a civilian authority.

MacArthur, who knew nothing of this, held a lavish reception on February 19, 1901, to celebrate his promotion and to introduce members of the new Federal Party to Manila. In what was a clear sign of his relief, he invited the members of the Philippine Commission and their wives to attend. The cold war between civilian and military sides thawed, at least for one night. The commissioners came, made polite conversation with MacArthur, and watched the cream of Manila society swirl around them. If a party could signal anything about the health of the occupation, this one did.

The Capture

What came next for the insurgents was disaster to compound catastrophe. Already reeling throughout the islands from the renewed American campaign, the insurrectos lost the man they believed more than anyone to be their representative and leader. Whatever his mistakes and frequent foolishness, Emilio Aguinaldo was, for many, the revolution personified. His armies might fall, but the Americans had been unable to kill or capture him—or even, after 1900, find him. As long as Aguinaldo stood, so stood the revolution.

He was not, however, to stand much longer. In early February 1901, Col. Frederick Funston, in San Isidro, received from one of his units a Filipino prisoner. The man—Cecilio Segismundo—claimed to be a courier for Aguinaldo, carrying encrypted messages. Funston's men, at the colonel's orders, encouraged the courier to reveal the meaning of the messages. How forceful this encouragement was remains ambiguous, but Segismundo revealed all he knew. Once translated and decrypted, the messages seemed to offer a spectacular intelligence windfall: the location of Emilio Aguinaldo. The president was hiding out in Palanan, in the northeast of Luzon, isolated from the rest of the Philippines by the desolate Sierra Madre mountain range. It was a good hiding place. The mountain passes were watched over by tribal warriors in the pay of the insurgents. They would warn of any force coming from that direction. In fact, exactly that had happened in 1899. An American column had marched through the mountains into Palanan. They found it deserted, for Aguinaldo and his men had fled quickly into the lower reaches of the mountains. The Americans, none the wiser, went on their way.

The sea was a different story, Funston realized. American control of the ocean gave him immediate and rapid access to the whole eastern coast of Luzon, despite the Sierra Madre. He could not steam directly into Palanan and hope to catch Aguinaldo. The smoke from the steam engines would give things away long before the Americans landed, and Funston did not want to repeat the experience of Young and Peyton back in March 1899, fruitlessly chasing Aguinaldo through a variety of terrain. But the ocean gave him the opportunity to be landed close to Aguinaldo and, if need be, taken off to safety immediately.

That would not be enough if Funston could not get to Aguinaldo before the president was warned and fled. Here another letter offered a possible way. The missive relayed a request to Aguinaldo's cousin Baldomero Aguinaldo to send reinforcements to Palanan. The president was short of troops.

Funston was due to be relieved within a few weeks, but this he could not ignore. What, he thought, if the troops coming in, acting as reinforcements, were actually disguised American forces? Could they capture Aguinaldo? Obviously, American soldiers would not do, but the buildup of native troops gave Funston another alternative.

He asked for permission from MacArthur for a daring attempt. He would take eighty-one native soldiers—scouts from the town of Macabebe in central Luzon—and dress them in captured insurgent uniforms. Then, along with himself and four other American officers pretending to be their captives, he would have this disguised force dropped by American gunboat on the east side of Luzon, near the town of Casiguran, twenty-seven miles north of the farthest American outpost at Baler. The force would march another hundred miles north along the coastline to Aguinaldo's location and attempt to capture the president and bring him back to Manila.

It was beyond daring. It was suicidal. But aggression and risk-taking by American officers had so long been rewarded that MacArthur hardly blinked an eye. He gave permission and off Funston went to plan. They were ready to go on March 6, 1901, sailing on the steamer *Vicksburg*. MacArthur saw Funston off at his Manila office with the encouraging words, "Funston, this is a desperate undertaking. I fear I shall never see you again." The Kansas general was not dissuaded.

Along with the Macabebe scouts, Funston had two brothers, Capt. R. T. Hazzard and Lt. O.P.M. Hazzard, both of the Eleventh Cavalry, U.S. Volunteers. In addition, and most crucial to the plan, Funston had a number of ex-insurgent officers, all of whom had been captured or surrendered, and all had come over to the American side. Perhaps most critical of these was Capt. Lasaro Segovia, an insulare who had fought in the Spanish army, then in the Army of Liberation, and finally, after giving himself up in May 1900, as a guide for the American army. Segovia had long experience in the archipelago and spoke both Spanish and Tagalog. The native courier, Segismundo, came with them to serve—either voluntarily or not—as a guide.

Funston's plan originally called for the expedition to find or purchase native boats to use in the landing. They did find some two-masted *bancas* at another town to use. Unfortunately, the bancas, while being towed behind the *Vicksburg*, sank in a storm, and Funston was forced to use the ship's boats instead. He landed at night, in hopes that no one would notice the American lines of the boats.

The landing went smoothly, and the *Vicksburg* sailed away, lurking offshore until a scheduled rendezvous off Palanan on March 25. Funston's force marched north through extremely challenging terrain. The mountains of the Sierra Madre sometimes descended directly into the ocean, forcing the American unit to scale cliffs and edge along precipices. It rained continuously and they were low on food.

But of all the things that could have gone wrong, the most important did not. The column managed to fool every insurgent they met, Funston relying heavily on the quick-witted Segovia to talk their way through the encounters. They reached Palanan about 3 p.m. on March 23 to find an honor guard of insurgents awaiting them. Segovia was with the lead party, while Funston and the other Americans were coming up behind them, to avoid causing suspicion on Aguinaldo's part. After some confusion, Segovia managed to get into the main headquarters and find Aguinaldo. He yelled at the Macabebes to open fire and raced upstairs to take the president prisoner. Funston recalled what followed:

> The Macabebes were so excited and nervous that their fire was very ineffective. But two of the insurgent soldiers were killed and the remainder in their flight threw away 18 rifles and 1000 rounds of ammunition.

Segovia shot two insurgent officers in the room with Aguinaldo and held the president captive until Funston arrived.[4]

It was the day after Aguinaldo's birthday, and the end of his war. The rendezvous with the *Vicksburg* went off without a hitch, and Funston shared the captain's mess with Commander Barry and Aguinaldo on the trip back to Manila. When they reached the city, Funston went directly to MacArthur's headquarters to announce the capture. MacArthur was overjoyed by the news. How best, he wondered, to take advantage of the coup? It was a military triumph, and could also be a political victory if he could use Aguinaldo against the remaining insurrectos. MacArthur's ideas ranged from the sensible, such as interrogating Aguinaldo and trying to get him to issue a proclamation of surrender, to the somewhat silly, such as having Aguinaldo go on a speaking tour of the United States.

Aguinaldo was a model guest. Though he thought Funston had played an "ungentlemanly and unsportsmanlike ruse," he was too worn down by the yearlong flight and the isolation of Palanan to offer much resistance.[5] The ilustrado took quickly to the comfort of his life of captivity. MacArthur put him in a cozy set of rooms to live in; from his second-story window he could watch American soldiers bloody themselves in impromptu games of football on the parade ground below.[6] He attended dinners with important Americans and Filipinos and his captors worked to convince him that further resistance was useless.

From Aguinaldo's insurgent comrades, the response was overwhelming dismay. In combination with the surrenders of other generals, his capture seemed a disastrous capstone. "We find ourselves, therefore, without a chief and without several of our old comrades. We who remain, shall we continue the struggle? Ought we to continue it? Can we continue it?" wrote the junta from Hong Kong on April 9.[7]

The Surrender

The insurgents had hardly had time to come to grips with the capture of Aguinaldo before the release on April 19 of a shattering message from their dictator-president. He had come around to MacArthur's point of view. We should spare a moment's sympathy for Aguinaldo. He had spent over a year on the run, frequently just barely ahead of the forces chasing him; he had seen his family members captured and taken away from him; and he had experienced the surrenders of his closest generals. Aguinaldo sensed grimly that the revolution was melting away from him:

> My capture, together with the treachery and betrayal that accompanied it, left me deeply angered, then distressed, then almost completely numbed. . . . I was overwhelmed by a feeling of disgust and despair.[8]

Vain, paranoid, militarily mostly incompetent, but with a keen sense of political survival, he decided that the best thing for Emilio Aguinaldo to do was to cooperate. "I also felt relieved. I had known for some time that our resistance was doomed to failure. . . . Now, it was over and I was alive."[9]

And cooperate he did, writing a general proclamation to his fellow insurrectos that the time had come to give up. "The complete termination of hostilities and a lasting peace are not only desirable but absolutely essential to the welfare of the Philippines," he wrote. "By acknowledging and accepting the sovereignty of the United States throughout the entire Archipelago, as I now do without any reservation whatsoever, I believe that I am serving thee, my beloved country." MacArthur had it published in English, Spanish, and Tagalog, and disseminated widely throughout the islands. It was capitulation. Aguinaldo, despite his lack of "reservations," would wear until his death in 1964 a black bow tie as a symbol of mourning for the Philippine Republic: a small enough tribute, perhaps.

The interesting thing is that it is not clear, for all his isolation, that Aguinaldo was wrong. The revolution was, in fact, melting away in spring 1901 under the high heat of the American offensive and continuing efforts at pacification. The insurgents had not been able to sustain their offensive of the fall, the election of 1900 had been a shattering blow to their morale, and American efforts had caused their supplies, most particularly food, to become extremely low. Aguinaldo's capture and surrender was not the turning point of the war, as many have argued. Rather, it was the final element of a turnaround that had started in December 1900.

That is not to say that much did not remain to be done after the spring of 1901. But the momentum had shifted clearly to the American side, and there was a growing sense within the U.S. administration, both in Manila and in Washington, D.C., that the civilian side of things—pacification and organization—would now dominate the Philippine effort. Even MacArthur recognized it. His dealings with Taft and the Philippine Commission had gone much more smoothly after the success of the winter-spring campaign. With the capture of Aguinaldo, MacArthur admitted to Taft that it was time for the commission to take over. He himself preferred not to remain as the military leader in that case, and between him, Taft, and Elihu Root, a compromise was worked out. The military would hand over supreme governing authority in the Philippines in July 1901 to the commission. Taft would become governor of the Philippines. At the same time, MacArthur would be relieved and brought home to the United States and replaced by Brig. Gen. Adna Chaffee, a veteran of the Civil War, the Indian Wars, and the China Expedition. Unlike MacArthur, Chaffee had risen from the ranks to his commission. The "mustang," as such officers were known, was blunt and plainspoken, unlike the departing general, whose circumlocutions had often been the source of mirth in Washington, D.C. Chaffee's office, Root made clear to all concerned, would be subordinate to Taft's except in provinces where the insurgency still flamed.

The Pacification Campaign

Before moving on to the middle of 1901, however, it is worth stopping a moment to look at the course of the pacification. American success and Filipino defeat in the guerrilla war came about as much because of the actions of hundreds of small units of soldiers and civilians in far-off isolated areas of the Philippines, as it did because of aggressive military campaigning. This was "small war" with a vengeance. American soldiers organized a civilian infrastructure on the ground that could run the Philippines effectively and, most critically, convince Filipino civilians that they should support American rule or, at least, not actively support the insurgents.

There were few grand victories in this campaign, few battles, and few dramatic turning points. Instead, the pacification campaign took place day by day and person by person. To get a sense of it, let us take a look at one of the people waging that war: Herbert Reddy, a corporal in the Sixth U.S. Volunteer Infantry Regiment in Mindanao.

During the spring of 1901, Corporal Reddy was told to train a squad of Filipinos. They spoke no English and he spoke nothing else. One of them, whose name Reddy reports as "Diablo," spoke a bit of Spanish. Reddy appointed him corporal of the squad for this language facility as well as for the fact that when Diablo read the attendance list, he, unlike Reddy, could pronounce their names. Training was difficult. The soldiers soon learned the English words for a variety of basic commands, and Reddy learned to turn his back to them when he showed them an element of the drill. If he faced them to demonstrate, for example, a salute, they would use the hand on the same side (left rather than right).[10]

After three months the squad was ready. The soldiers took the oath of allegiance, and, with Reddy still commanding, were sent to garrison a small port in northern Mindanao. There he was the law. He "was in charge of camp, postoffice, sanitation, and also captain of the port. When a boat came in, just any kind of boat, the owner or captain had to bring his log to me to show from where it came, and what it carried. To make sure, I had to check the cargo." But few boats stopped by.[11]

Reddy reports participating in no battles or combat. He and his men served as a guard for a group of Moros evacuating their wounded after a battle between them and a group of Christian Filipinos. After their return, Reddy decided that his men "deserved something other than the hard tack and canned beef we'd been living on," so he took his native guide and set out to find some fresh meat. On their travels, they came across a tiny, impoverished settlement:

> We came into a little clearing in which, near the center, some trees had been left standing. In them were some crude nests—I couldn't call them huts—in which we found three families. The poor little frightened black people had nothing to eat except what they garnered from the jungle.

The families were scared of him until he "made [them] understand that we were in search of food, not of them, and went on." Eventually, he found some villagers who agreed to butcher a cow and sell him the meat. From them, Reddy acquired strips of beef and fresh eggs to bring back to his men. On his way back he stopped in the clearing again and gave the poor tree dwellers some of the beef. And, he said proudly, "my men feasted."[12]

One day during Reddy's stint, a boat showed up in the harbor and landed two men with "heavy suitcases." They were teachers sent by Manila to open a school of English for the local children. But there was no place for them to stay in the village. Reddy offered them a room in the house being used by the troops, at the discount price of twenty-five dollars per month "in advance." The teachers accepted, and when Reddy got the first month's rent, he "went to the Chinese store and purchased two dozen porcelain plates, cups, and saucers, and also knives, forks, and spoons. Twenty four mess kits went into haversacks and were hung on the wall."[13]

None of this was high drama. None of this rose to the attention of Arthur MacArthur or William Taft, let alone the government in Washington, D.C. A commanding officer fed both his troops and some impecunious natives. He established a trading bond with other natives, both Filipino and Chinese. He regulated and organized the trade of the local port. He helped the local Moros deal with their wounded. He treated his native soldiers well. He helped (albeit at a profit) set up a local school. It wasn't spectacular, but, writ large, it was crucial. America's control of the Philippines was built on hundreds if not thousands of similar situations. The conflict consisted not merely of combat, but of a whole set of activities along the broad spectrum that had politics at one end and war at the other. And it was successful, more or less. Combined with the military campaigns and the failures of the insurgent forces, the pacification efforts had the essential effect of sucking necessary oxygen out of the revolution.

Some American soldiers integrated themselves into Filipino society so successfully that they decided to stay when their enlistments ended. Enlistees had the choice of accepting their discharge either in the Philippines or at home in the United States, and it appears that quite a few took them in the Philippines. For many, the Philippines were an attractive place to settle. They had grown to understand the culture and speak—at least adequately—the languages. Many soldiers started relationships with native women. These women were sometimes called *queridas* (lovers) and sometimes, in another echo of the American West, "squaws."[14] For African-American soldiers the islands were particularly attractive. The Filipinos, though ruled by white Americans, were largely a people of color. In addition, their army pensions gave them an economic position that far surpassed that of most African-Americans in the United States. "In this country will be many fortunes made," wrote William F. Blakeny, a soldier in the Twenty-fifth Infantry Regiment, to the *Indianapolis Freeman* on January 24, 1902. "Why not come and share with us the glorious good times which are sure to come? Come now."[15]

Despite all of this, of course, the war was not over. The insurgency had been dealt a severe blow. That it was mortal would not become obvious for many months. The surrenders of the spring months had made clear the success of MacArthur's offensive and general plan. But, as always, the rainy season would enforce a suspension of active military campaigning, if not of pacification efforts, and only the arrival of the fall would tell if the insurgency could recover itself. American commanders had considered the war over once before. They would not make the same mistake twice.

The highlight of the rainy season was, of course, the handover of governing power from the U.S. Army to the Philippine Commission. It happened, for all the right patriotic reasons, on July 4, 1901. Earlier that week, Taft had held a farewell reception for Arthur MacArthur and had even courteously escorted him down to his waiting steamer. Only an ungracious mind would suspect that the Ohio politician was making sure that the general did leave the archipelago for good.

He did. To be fair to both Taft and MacArthur, despite their difficulties, they never admitted in public the friction that had dogged them, even when, as in their testimony before a Senate committee in 1902, they had ample opportunity to do so. Moreover, Taft found that Chaffee, though perhaps never rising to the heights of MacArthur, could be troublesome in his own right. But the lines of authority were much more clearly drawn after July 1901. Taft was the man in charge and Chaffee, while still enjoying a fair amount of room to maneuver, never had the sort of proconsular authority that MacArthur did. A U.S. general would not be in that kind of position as an American Caesar again until Douglas MacArthur accepted Japan's surrender on the deck of the battleship *Missouri* in September 1945 and became that nation's de facto ruler.

Taft quickly set about adding a strong Filipino presence at every level of the American government. He wished to give the Filipinos as much responsibility as they could handle, always, of course, under the paternal and guiding hand of the United States. He increased, with Chaffee's grudging assent, the size of the Philippine constabulary. He added three Filipino members to the Philippine Commission itself, giving the native population a voice (albeit one that could be outvoted by the American commissioners) in the highest levels of government. With the insurgency winding down, it was time to look to the long-term governance of the islands.

Difficulties in the Fall

As always, however, American plans went awry in the first few months after the end of the rainy season. September 1901 witnessed a series of events that unsettled American efforts domestically and in the archipelago, and ensured that the war was unlikely to end that year.

First, and most importantly, was the assassination of William McKinley. We should remember that presidential assassinations were not an uncommon occurrence in the late nineteenth century. Presidents Lincoln and Garfield had both been shot to death while in office, meaning that before McKinley and after the start of the Civil War, two out of eight presidents had been murdered. One member of the McKinley administration, Secretary of State John Hay, had, in fact, served in the governments of both Lincoln and Garfield, and had been around for both their assassinations. It was his misfortune to be around for a third presidential killing.

We should also remember that the presidency was a different office, with a different role, in the late nineteenth century. The presidents before McKinley were not surrounded by the layers of administration and security that characterized the twentieth century. Grover Cleveland would often walk by himself around Washington, unrecognized and unthreatened. McKinley increased the administrative layers, but not particularly the security, of the office of the president.

Thus, when President McKinley visited the Pan-American Exposition in Buffalo, New York, on September 6, 1901, he was not protected by a phalanx of Secret Service men. As he stood in a receiving line shaking hands, Leon Czolgosz stepped forward and, using a revolver he had concealed under a handkerchief, shot the president twice in the chest. Czolgosz was a mentally unbalanced hanger-on of the American anarchist movement. Estranged from his family, he had been inspired by the assassination of King Umberto I of Italy by an anarchist in 1900.

The revolver was chambered for a .32-caliber round. This was a relatively low-powered bullet, and McKinley, though he collapsed when he was shot, rallied quickly and seemed on the mend. "Good news from the President," presidential adviser Charles Dawes wrote in his diary on September 8. "The President continues to improve," he wrote two days later. The situation seemed safe enough for Dawes to leave Buffalo and return to Washington. But McKinley's condition turned for the worse. An infection set in, likely caused by the fragments of cloth and skin carried into the wounds by the bullets, and on September 13, Dawes was awakened at 4 a.m. to read a telegram in Washington warning him that the president was going through a "sinking spell." Dawes hurried back to Buffalo, reaching the president's bedside that evening. There he found McKinley surrounded by his family, fading rapidly. In the absence of antibiotics, there was little to do except watch and hope. The vigil continued throughout the evening. "Once, he said 'Oh dear,' as if in distress," Dawes remembered, but other than that the president did not speak. At 2:15 a.m. on September 14, McKinley died.

And so Mark Hanna's greatest fear at the Republican National Convention had come true: "that damned cowboy is President of the United States."[16] Theodore Roosevelt— "that damned cowboy"—was vacationing in the Adirondacks when McKinley was shot. The weather was bad, and Roosevelt decided to stay put unless the president took a turn for the worse. Two telegrams reaching him on September 13 convinced him of the need to leave. The first announced McKinley's sinking condition and ended with the unambiguous words "ABSOLUTELY NO HOPE." The second, from the cabinet, suggested that Roosevelt should "LOSE NO TIME COMING."[17] Roosevelt rode overnight out of the mountains, through pouring rain, to reach the nearest train station. His secretary had commissioned a special train for him, and it carried Roosevelt first to Albany and then Buffalo, reaching the city the same day as McKinley's death.

He was inaugurated that afternoon at a private house in Buffalo. Elihu Root spoke for the cabinet, pausing to struggle with tears. Roosevelt was sworn in by Judge John Hazel and in brief remarks to the assembled cabinet, politicians, and newspaper reporters, promised to "continue absolutely unbroken the policy of President McKinley for the peace, prosperity, and the honor of our beloved country." Root, in a brief quiet conversation earlier, had suggested the phrasing. Roosevelt was forty-two years old, the youngest president to that date in American history.[18] He walked back alone to his hotel room after the inauguration, refusing the security of a police escort.

The new president of the United States, never shy, set about stamping his own mark on the office. He mostly lived up to the promise to continue McKinley's policies, but Roosevelt's personality was too large and too outgoing to be contained within the withdrawn shell that McKinley had perfected. Roosevelt lived the office, as he had lived so many roles before, and there was some adjustment required on behalf of all parties concerned. Roosevelt was even more fervently committed to the Philippine project than had been McKinley. His imperialism was heart-felt and ongoing, though he came to the presidency just as the conflict seemed to be winding down.

The news of the McKinley assassination made it to Manila by the middle of September and slowly trickled to American outposts throughout the islands over the rest of the month. In late September it reached the island of Samar and then on to the town of Balangiga, where Company C of the Ninth U.S. Volunteer Infantry Regiment was stationed. The company reacted with sadness, and flew the American flag at half mast to signal their mourning.

Balangiga was a small town on the south coast of a province that had not yet been declared pacified. The insurgent leader there, Gen. Vincente Lukban, had proven aggressive and able, and had managed to continue his resistance even as so many others were surrendering. In June an American patrol lost in the interior of Samar was ambushed and took heavy casualties. The island gained a reputation as a fierce and dangerous place, and activities there spilled over into the adjacent island of Leyte, separated by only a few hundred yards of open water.

The American response on Samar had been stringent, including the burning of crops, the slaughter of domestic animals, and the concentration of the locals into guarded zones. The combination of tactics had brought the population dangerously close to starvation by the fall of 1901, and district heads were forced to import rice to stave off potential deaths.

Company C had run into some difficulties from the start. Capt. Thomas W. Connell, the company commander, enforced fairly stringent discipline on the natives as soon as the troops arrived. Wanting to clear an area around the town and garrison, he took a number of hostages to get the villagers and surrounding Filipinos to work at cleaning up the town and clearing the brush.

On September 27, the insurgents, led by Lt. Col. Eugenio Daza, armed largely with bolos, sneaked into the church next to the company's mess area. Daza also managed to infiltrate a number of insurrectos into the hostages the Americans had taken. That done, the insurgents waited for a good moment to spring an ambush. The next morning, when the lion's share of the company was eating breakfast without their rifles, the insurgents struck, spilling out of the church and the tents and setting upon the unsuspecting American troops.

It was a textbook success for the Filipinos. The attack came suddenly enough that the soldiers did not realize immediately what was happening. Cpl. Ernest Manire had just filled his mess plate with hash when the commotion broke out. He asked the man next to him, Sergeant Martin, what was going on. "He could not answer, as he was split through the head obliquely towards the left shoulder with a bolo."[19]

With the surprise, and at such close range, the insurgent

disadvantage in weapons was neutralized, and bitter hand-to-hand combat broke out. The soldiers fought back with whatever they could, Pvt. G. E. Meyer remembered: "clubs, baseball bats, pots, bolos—anything they could lay hold of. . . . I saw Private Degraffenreid, a great big fellow, standing on a pile of rocks, which he was hurling at the natives, bowling them over like nine pins."

In addition to going after the soldiers, the insurgents also sought out American weapons, but they were hindered by the fact that many could not operate captured Krag-Jorgensen rifles effectively. The rifle had a five-round magazine and a bolt action. It could be fired and loaded in two ways. In the first way, working the bolt would bring another round from the magazine into the chamber and ready the rifle to be fired immediately. In the second way, if the "lockout" was activated, working the bolt would open the chamber, but not load another round, relying instead on the operator to hand-load another cartridge. The idea was to hand-load and fire, while keeping the magazine in reserve. Many of the rifles were set in this position, and the natives did not understand how to deactivate the lockout, limiting them to the slower rate of fire. But it was more important for the insurgents to prevent the Americans from recovering their rifles, and this they did. They detailed a strong force to cover the American barracks, where most of the rifles were, and when the soldiers raced to get their weapons, the Americans were cut down.

The American soldiers got much the worst of it. Meyer remembered the scene:

> The dead and dying [lay] all around. I particularly remember one man bleeding from a gaping wound in his

forehead, sitting bolt upright on the ladder in front of
our shack, dying. . . . Private J. J. Driscoll was crawling
on his hands and feet like a stabbed pig, his brains
falling out through a wound he had received.

Connell and his second in command, Lt. Edward Bumpus,
were killed in the first rush, and the soldiers that remained
were dazed, scattered, and often wounded. "My ears,"
Meyer continued, "were filled with the pitiful cries of our
wounded and dying, pleading for help, some trying to stop
the flow of blood with dry dirts and pieces of their shirts.
. . . I saw Sergeant Martin seated at the table leaning forward with a spoon clutched in his hand and his head cut
completely off."[20] Some of the soldiers sought refuge in the
water of the bay, but the insurgents chased them out in
boats and stabbed them until they sank and drowned. "The
surprise and force of the attack," Col. E. G. Peyton later
wrote in the postmortem, "was so thoroughly carried out
that all the officers and more than half of the enlisted men
were killed or severely wounded during the first few min-
utes."[21]

Some of the Americans won the race to get to the rifles,
and they, mostly, survived. Most did not, and they, mostly,
did not. The first attack killed over forty American soldiers.
Of the twenty-six that remained alive, twenty-four were
wounded, some severely. They managed to gather near the
beach and establish a defensive position. But they quickly
realized that they could not stay. The insurgents were numerous, they controlled the town and the American camp,
and the surviving soldiers had no food or water.

What they did have were boats, and the remnants of
Company C decided to board the boats and escape the

town. They managed to load up the vessels and set off, with canoes full of insurgents chasing. But long-range rifle fire from the Americans induced the enemy to stay at a distance. After several days at sea, with limited food and water and suffering from the sun and salt, the men made it to the nearest American outpost at Basey. There they were treated, and the gunboat *Pittsburgh* was sent on a relief expedition back to Balangiga. When it arrived, it found the town abandoned but for dead American bodies. The final toll was forty-eight American soldiers killed. By contrast, the insurgents lost between twenty-five and thirty dead and a similar number wounded.

The soldiers who survived, even unwounded, were traumatized by the sights they had seen. Experiences from the attack remained "vividly stamped" in the minds of the soldiers. Meyer would remember long afterward the "ghastly panoramas of my butchered messmates." Cpl. Arnold Irish "used to have the most terrible nightmares, always fighting the natives, and finally I had a nervous breakdown and brain fever combined."[22]

Vengeance

The reaction to the attack was immediate and telling. The slaughter was the worst loss of life the American army experienced in a single incident during the war, and it came at a time when the insurgency seemed to be ending. It seemed somehow illicit; didn't the Filipinos understand that they were beaten? Part of this reaction can be seen in the label the attack was given. It was not called a battle or a skirmish or a loss, but the Balangiga *massacre*, and the implication of a sly, wanton, treacherous assault by ungrateful natives is clear. Hosts of legends sprang up around the attack: that 250 insurgents had been killed by the Americans and that the insurgents had mutilated the dead bodies of the American soldiers were only two out of many. In reality, however, the attack at Balangiga was just that: an attack. It was carried out skillfully by the insurgents led by Daza and resulted in an overwhelming military victory for them.

Manila acted immediately. The town of Balangiga was razed to the ground, such that nothing there remains to this day but the bare walls of the church used to conceal the ambushers. General Chaffee organized a special unit, the Sixth Separate Brigade, to send to the island and once and for all end the insurgency there.

In command, he appointed Gen. Jacob Hurd Smith, a Civil War veteran who had been in the army ever since. He had had, by any definition, a checkered career. Smith started off well, fighting valiantly in the Civil War. Shot at the Battle of Shiloh, he carried a Minié ball from that engagement in one hip for the rest of his life. But, much like Gen. George Patton in later years, Smith was not good outside active combat. While recuperating from his wound he served as a recruiting officer for the remaining three years of the Civil War. Smith illegally used money from recruiting bounties to invest in a variety of private firms, and saw his wealth grow rapidly.

Despite the newfound money, after the Civil War he encountered the same career stagnation that so many others had. Smith did not take to the situation well. He showed a tendency to write imprudent things to senior officers, which led to a series of courts-martial. After a guilty verdict in one of these during the 1880s, Smith was cashiered from the army. Reinstated by the intervention of Grover Cleveland, Smith mostly behaved himself in the 1890s, perhaps scared by the nearness of his escape.

The Spanish-American War returned him to the fighting: he did well at the Battle of El Caney in Cuba, getting shot in the chest in the process. Coming over to the Philippines, he served under MacArthur in the central Luzon campaign and again distinguished himself to the commanding general. MacArthur recommended him for promotion to brigadier general in early 1901, a recommendation that Taft agreed with, though with the ambiguous caveat that Smith "has reached a time when promotion . . . would worthily end his services, for I believe that it is his intention to retire upon promotion."[23]

This was wishful thinking. Smith accepted the promotion and continued his career, and when the situation on Samar arose, Chaffee appointed him commander of the Sixth Separate Brigade without hesitation. Historians have remembered this as a bad decision, and it was.[24] But Smith's actions on Samar, while extreme, were initially spurred on and encouraged by the American command, both military and civilian. It was time, all agreed, for harshness on Samar.

Smith is reported to have told his subordinates to turn the interior of the island into a "howling wilderness," and to execute all male inhabitants of the island over the age of ten. How serious Smith was when he said it remains in some doubt, but the general stringency of his policies is not. Smith tightened a vise on Samar by land and sea. A naval blockade closed around the island. American gunboats captured or sank boats moving without a license from the American command. By the end of 1901, 226 ships and boats had been so treated. On land, the population was forced into zones of concentration around the major towns and anything left outside was considered fair game. American units burned villages, killed animals, and destroyed crops.

Worse, the American presence in Samar in late 1901 and early 1902 was marked by vicious brutality in too many instances. A fair number of American officers, encouraged explicitly or implicitly by Smith, tortured and executed insurrectos, prisoners, and civilians without evidence or trial. Though many officers attempted to mitigate Smith's orders and avoid cruelty, many did not. It may not have been a howling wilderness, but it was still bad. William Keane, who took part in the campaign, recalled, "We did not take any prisoners. We shot everybody on sight."[25] That this was largely an aberration in the American effort does not excuse it.

Things were bad enough by the beginning of 1902 that Taft insisted Chaffee do something. The commanding general sailed down to Samar in January and spent several weeks there, insisting that Smith drastically scale back the violence and depredations. He did so, and Samar began, to an extent, to recover. This recovery was aided in May and June by the surrender of General Lukban and the general collapse of the insurgency.[26] By the summer of 1902, the insurgency on the island had been crushed for the most part. The rebel bands that remained were scattered, ill-equipped, and incapable of serious action. American rule, for the most part, was unchallenged. The stringency had worked, at some cost in pain and suffering. How much of that suffering was unnecessary will never be known.

Cholera

The tactics of civilian concentration had been successful on Samar, as they had been elsewhere. But they had created a dangerous situation that finally came to a head in 1902. Cramming thousands together at close quarters in areas without sufficient capacity led to extreme problems with sanitation and hygiene. An army surgeon remarked on the situation:

> I find excreta, dead animals, slop, stable manure, and other filth made by the Army have been dumped from 100 to 300 yards from the spring which furnishes drinking water for the entire town. . . . I am surprised that any office should have allowed such vile filth to be dumped on ground where it is liable to contaminate the water supply.[27]

The unsanitary conditions often combined with a lack of sufficient food, as farmers were unable to bring in their crops for want of field hands to harvest them or because the crops were destroyed by American units. The result was a tightly packed, somewhat malnourished population with severe sanitation problems and compromised immune systems, a perfect situation for an epidemic.

That it did not occur in 1901 can be laid to the weather. The concentration policy did not really gather steam until the fall, and the cooler weather of the fall and winter slowed down disease transmission. But with the warming of spring 1902, all the above factors came into play. The result was a catastrophic outbreak of disease.

The culprit was cholera, a disease spread through contaminated food and water. Once ingested, cholera bacteria take up residence in the small intestine. The toxins they give off cause the intestinal walls to leak fluid, leading to an extreme case of diarrhea, vomiting, and massive dehydration. Without rehydration, the person soon dies of water and electrolyte loss.

Prevention requires extensive sanitation efforts and a commitment to personal and societal hygiene. Treatment in the current day is rehydration using a combination of intravenous fluid and electrolytes, antibiotics to shorten the course of the disease, and rest. Today, cholera is considered a rare but easily treatable disease. In the Philippines at the turn of the century it was a death warrant. Antibiotics had not been invented, and the need for rehydration was not understood clearly. Nor was rehydration straightforward. The supply of sterile water was low, given the large quantities needed, and it was difficult to produce enough of it by boiling.

George C. Marshall was then a young lieutenant, just graduated from the Virginia Military Institute, who was journeying to his unit in the Philippines. He arrived in Manila to find it wracked by the disease. That slowed his journey substantially; though he could leave the city on an interisland steamer, he had to sit on the ship for five days as it anchored offshore of Mindoro, under quarantine. After the passage of five days made it clear that no one on board had the illness, Marshall landed. But it was only a month or so before cholera broke out there. It started with extraordinary suddenness. Marshall remembered meeting three nuns early one May morning and chatting with them briefly. Then:

I mention these sisters in particular because suddenly the cholera broke out. It broke out almost in a day. We had no warning of it there. We thought we were safe. It broke out and the three sisters—I helped bury them by three o'clock that afternoon.[28]

The soldiers had no means of curing the disease. All they could do was watch the natives suffer and attempt to prevent transmission.

The outbreak was severe enough that they were hard-pressed not to fall victim to it themselves. The army enforced strict hygiene, as Marshall remembered:

Spread not by contact with the sick, but by contamination of food and drink, [cholera] could be checked by meticulous cleanliness. Men in Calapan were confined to barracks; everything they ate or drank was thoroughly boiled; hands had to be scrubbed, mess kits scoured and thoroughly rinsed. These procedures were rigorously enforced by military discipline lest the soldiers, like soldiers everywhere, took shortcuts. A very little skimping could cost you your life.[29]

Marshall's unit set up a "cholera isolation camp" for the sick Filipinos, in hopes of reducing the spread of the disease. There, the only constant was death, as Marshall found when he visited:

The first time I went I found the soldiers [on guard] peacefully eating their supper off a pile of coffins. Later on, there weren't any coffins. The deaths came too rap-

idly and they were buried by dozens in a trench. A sheet
was put over them and disinfectant poured on them. It
was a tragic sight. The sides of the tents were rolled up
so you could see the patients on these gold metal cots
without any sheets, their legs drawn up almost under
their chins, generally shrieking from the agony of con-
vulsions. But they didn't last long. . . . I don't remember
anybody recovering at that time.[30]

The Americans were trying. Marshall worked himself to
exhaustion during the epidemic. One evening he was chatting with a doctor friend named Fletcher Gardener, who
emphasized a point by saying that he believed he had come
down with cholera and was going to die. Marshall then
dozed off in the middle of the conversation. The next
morning he woke up to see Gardener, who did not have
cholera, but shook his fist at the young lieutenant and
mockingly shouted, "There's the damn fellow who went to
sleep when I told him I was dying."[31]

There was nothing funny about the epidemic. It hit
some areas particularly hard. The densely populated parts
of central Luzon had a high casualty rate, as did the southern province of the Batangas. But all the provinces were affected to one degree or another. Exactly how many died is
difficult to figure precisely. Those who died, as we have seen
from Marshall's remembrances, were often simply laid out
in mass graves without record. The only population counts
from the pre-American period are deeply unreliable Spanish
censuses, which makes comparisons to post-epidemic censuses less than useful. But the most plausible estimates for
cholera deaths seem to be in the range of 150,000 to
200,000. The result was a demographic catastrophe that re-

sembled the ones of the 1880s, the decade of death, as it had been called.

The last year of the war should thus be seen against this background. Even as the insurgents fought to sustain themselves and hold on to the last remnants of their revolution, hundreds of thousands of their compatriots were dying. They themselves suffered greatly from the illness and a large number surrendered while sick, or simply died in their refuges, disappearing from the fight without recollection or record. Even as the Americans sought to chase the insurgents, hundreds of thousands of their new subjects died, and a fair number of U.S. soldiers fell prey to the disease.

Thus, even as the embers of the fight flickered only fitfully, the conflict—colored by the atrocities of Samar and the wave of cholera—took a darker, more apocalyptic hue. The Philippines seemed to be collapsing into barbarity and chaos, compounded by a locust swarm that accompanied the cholera epidemic in a number of provinces. The situation seemed biblical, and the book of choice, Revelations.

Domestic Reaction

It did not take long for news of Jacob Smith's actions on Samar to trickle back to North America. The horror of the situation confirmed for many anti-imperialists what they had been warning about all along. The United States would not civilize the Filipinos; instead, the situation would see Americans descend into cruelty and callousness. In response, the anti-imperialists raised a storm of protest.

The most concrete form of this was the convening of hearings in the Senate to examine events in the Philippines. That politics played a role is undoubtedly true; the 1902 midterm elections were looming, and the Democrats sensed vulnerability in a Republican Party shocked by the loss of its leader and still coming to terms with Theodore Roosevelt. The committee members were aided by the secret intriguing of the ambitious commanding general of the U.S. Army, Nelson A. Miles. Miles, appointed to the largely ceremonial post in 1895, had felt continually slighted by first Root and McKinley and then Root and Roosevelt. The resentment had festered in the fall of 1901 when a number of indiscreet comments on Miles's part had led to both private and public rebukes by the secretary of war and the president and included a confrontation with Roosevelt at a White House reception in December. Miles saw his opportunity in the Philippine situation to wreak political revenge on the administration, and he worked behind the scenes to do so.

But to ascribe all or even most of the motivation to politics is grievously to underestimate the genuine concerns that senators like George Frisbie Hoar of Massachusetts had. He believed that empire was utterly incompatible with the spirit of the American republic and here, he worried, was confirmation.

The hearings started on January 26, 1902, before the cholera outbreak reached epidemic levels. They were held in private, without much publicity, a surer sign of the lack of political calculation than any assurance the senators made. For months, a parade of witnesses, including Elwell Otis and Arthur MacArthur, sat in front of the Senate committee to testify about the situation in the Philippines.

Even as this searching examination was taking place behind closed doors, the public news from the archipelago continued to be unsettling. Cholera deaths were one thing;

another was the full flowering of the results of Samar. A series of trials drove home to the American public the violence and brutality committed there. First in the docket was William Littleton Waller, a Marine major who, after a disastrous reconnaissance mission that might have served Joseph Conrad well for a model, had summarily ordered the execution of eleven native guides for no more real crime than assisting Marines starving in the jungles of Samar. Put in front of a court-martial, Waller defended himself with reference to General Order 100. Things might have remained confined to that, but the prosecution put Jacob Smith on the stand, and the general essentially perjured himself in denying the orders he had given his subordinates. Smith's testimony was swiftly rebutted by a series of witnesses, leading to Waller's exoneration. Next in the docket was Smith himself, his court-martial ordered by Roosevelt personally.

What emerged from the court-martial to a distressed America was a catalog of questionable behavior. For the first time, the grimy details of the campaign in Samar became public and the public did not like what it saw. Combined with the release of information from the Senate hearings on the Philippines, the result was a political firestorm centered on Elihu Root and Theodore Roosevelt. "If we are to 'benevolently assimilate' Filipinos by such methods, we should frankly so state, and drop our canting hypocrisy about having to wage war on these people for their own betterment," wrote *The Times-Picayune* (New Orleans).[32]

Roosevelt's difficulties were compounded by the timing. The postassassination honeymoon period was well over by the spring of 1902 and Republican thoughts were beginning to turn to the midterm elections and the presidential race of 1904. Large sections of the GOP were not convinced that Roosevelt was the man to lead them in either the short or long term. To replace him, they hoped to convince a man of eminence, popularity, and unquestioned ties to the policies of McKinley: Sen. Mark Hanna.

Outrage over the Philippines thus hit Roosevelt at his most vulnerable. From the start, he had been clearly identified with the imperial adventure in both the Philippines and Cuba. He had played a large role in getting the nation involved in the Philippines, from war planning with the Asiatic fleet, to the telegram message of February 25, 1898, sending Dewey to Manila Bay, to the unstinting support he had expressed in the years afterward. A substantial chunk of his public popularity had come from his exploits in Cuba. He saw himself as a new breed of Republican, carrying the United States forward into a twentieth century of American power and prominence. The weakness of this was, of course, the suspicion of the old-line Republican establishment, personified by the man who might now take his place on the Republican ticket.

Roosevelt went on the counteroffensive. A series of articles in Republican newspapers condemned the criticism and minimized the atrocities. The capstone of the effort was a speech by Roosevelt's close friend Henry Cabot Lodge in the Senate on May 5. In it, the senator admitted that American soldiers had committed atrocities and expressed regret over their actions. But, Lodge pointed out, atrocities had occurred on both sides. He went on to list a catalog of horrors visited on Americans by the insurrectos, listing a variety of dismemberments, mutilations, and other vicious acts. American atrocities, he concluded, may not have occurred "altogether without provocation."[33]

The counterattack was enough to moderate the storm.

Further moderation occurred after the results of Smith's court-martial. His legal counsel had been smart enough to keep the general off the stand, and thus prevented him from making further imprudent statements. Though Smith was found guilty, it was only of using improvident language to his subordinates, and the court gave as punishment only an admonition. To that, Roosevelt added involuntary retirement. The result did not please those at the far ends of the argument, but for most it was enough, and the furor settled down and allowed Congress to debate and pass a permanent government act for the Philippines.

That act organized the American infrastructure in the islands for the long term. The post of military governor would be abolished, and the governor of the islands would be a civilian, if still supported by the continuing presence of American forces. With the insurgency flickering out, the risk of turning the entire government over to civilian administrators was relatively minimal. The situation had changed since the fall of 1901, and there was little to suggest that the insurgents could make anything that resembled a concerted effort.

The government act was passed in July 1902, giving Roosevelt the opportunity to issue a proclamation declaring an end to the conflict on July 4. The date, obvious in its symbolism, was well timed for the run-up to the 1902 midterm elections. It also put the final capstone on any discussion of American atrocities. The war was over, Roosevelt was saying implicitly, and now was the time to move forward. As a final sop, Roosevelt included in the proclamation an amnesty offer to any insurrectos still active who wished to surrender themselves.

Roosevelt's proclamation, of course, had no actual effect

on the ground. There was still fighting going on, and there would be for years to come. The Americans could call those attacking them whatever they wished, as Pvt. Evan Wyatt did in December 1902 when talking about an ambush suffered by his unit. Wyatt's detachment was marching through the jungle. Warned of a Filipino band, they attempted to preempt an assault but, "not knowing the exact location, we marched right into them, and they opened fire and got three of us on the first volley." Wyatt himself was wounded in the arm, but kept firing. Gradually, the Americans recovered. "The enemy retreated, but kept firing. We followed them for some distance, firing at every one we saw . . . and I continued with the boys till the firing stopped and the chase was ended." The ambush strongly resembled any number of insurgent assaults during the war, but Wyatt was careful to note that this was a "band of outlaws," not insurgents.[34]

So some of this was semantics. But such semantics nonetheless reflected a reality on the ground. Guerrilla wars rarely end with a climactic moment or a definitive battle. No bang, but rather the whimper of slow attrition. By July 1902, the insurrectos had lost most of their leadership and the bulk of their soldiers. Perhaps most importantly, they could no longer manage to attack the Americans with any kind of sustained intensity. In retrospect, Balangiga had been the last effective blow rather than the start of a new campaign. In a conventional war, there would have been someone to surrender the effort, to explicitly end the war. In the guerrilla campaign, the clearest mark of victory was that there was no one left to surrender the flag of the Philippine Republic.

Conclusion

A MOST FAVORED RACE

The war was over. What remained, in the aftermath, was the peace. The Filipinos, of different religions, ethnicities, and ideas, had to figure out a way to live with their new imperial overlords. The Americans, for their part, had to figure out how to rule their first colony. Early signs were not promising. Though Roosevelt declared that the war had ended in July 1902, sporadic resistance continued for more than a decade, and the American army undertook major campaigns in Leyte and Samar from 1905 to 1907 and in Cavite Province in 1905. Fighting against the Moros continued until 1913. In 1911, army strategists assumed that upon the start of a war between the United States and another power in the Pacific, "insurrection of the native population" would occur "quite generally."[1] But in fact that evaluation was almost exactly wrong. What is remarkable is how quickly both sides found out how to live together peaceably, to the point that even after Philippine independence in 1946, a remarkably strong alliance, political and cultural, endured between the United States and the Philippines.

Part of the reason for that smoothness was the simple fact that many of the same people were ruling the Philippines before and after the arrival of the Americans. The local elites in many cases had come to an accommodation with the Americans, either early or late in the process. Gen. Daniel Tirona had done so in the fall of 1899, an early convert to American rule; Aguinaldo himself had done so in the spring of 1901; and even holdouts like Miguel Malvar came around in early 1902. As these elites negotiated their surrender to American rule, they were in essence agreeing to integration rather than submission. For the most part, despite their opposition to American forces, they remained part of the power structure in their areas, and were allowed to continue their economic, political, and social dominance.

The result was a fairly rapid adjustment on both sides. The American government in the Philippines used a relatively light touch in its rule, and included a fair range of Filipino voices in its administration. It was nowhere near a representative government and the great mass of the Filipinos remained confined by economic and political bonds, but it was more than an imperial government that ruled by fiat and force majeure.

The Filipinos, in fact, became something of a "favored race" in American eyes. By the 1920s they were a culturally acceptable minority, an ethnic group viewed with condescending approval rather than simple contempt. Most Asians were regarded by the United States with great suspicion: immigration from China and Japan was severely curtailed in the 1910s and 1920s. Filipinos did not experience that same organized exclusion. Thus, for example, in 1923, when the U.S. Navy reopened recruitment after years of post–World War I cutbacks, it continued to forbid the enlistment of African-Americans. In their place as mess stewards and assistants, Filipinos were brought in. They enjoyed the status of an inferior but favored race.

For their part, the Filipinos seem to have shared a general acceptance of, and even affection for, American rule. By the time World War II started, four decades later, Filipino loyalties proved to be—pretty unswervingly—to the Americans. The rapid Japanese victories in 1941–42 did not sway the inhabitants of the archipelago to the side of Nippon; nor did a determined Japanese propaganda campaign to portray the Americans as imperial overlords and themselves as liberators.

Instead, the Filipinos, after the flight of Gen. Douglas MacArthur and the surrender of the last American garrison on Corregidor Island, started another guerrilla war, one that they sustained for the four years of Japanese occupation. They fought, and they waited for MacArthur's promised return. Contrast that with the situation in India, where the British found that the threat of Japanese invasion either had little effect on colonial populations or actually encouraged anti-British defiance. Thus, Mahatma Gandhi refused to help defend India for the British, and other anti-British Indians formed the Indian National Army, a force that aimed to overthrow British rule with the help of the Japanese.

During this time, there was never any move to make the

Philippines a U.S. state—race and nationalism made sure
of that—but they were much more than a colony, and the
Philippines' postwar independence seemed right to everyone, American and Filipino together. It was the just reward
for loyalty. For that, and for being raised up, the Filipinos
felt in many ways that they owed the United States. As
Reynaldo Ileto wrote, Filipino perception was that the Filipinos "owed a lifelong inner debt, or *utang na loób*" to
" 'Mother America.' "[2]

That America's presence in the Philippines had originated in violence and bloodshed was, if not forgotten, at
least set aside. The Philippine-American War became something of a lost history during most of the twentieth century,
as the two sides in that war found themselves working and
living together amicably. So amicable was the negotiation
that Filipino revolutionary symbols could easily be appropriated for an American audience, without a ripple of dis-
content on either side. In the 1945 John Wayne film *Back
to Bataan*, the Wayne character, left behind by American
forces, helps lead a guerrilla war against the Japanese occu-
piers with the help of a valiant Filipino, played by Anthony
Quinn. Quinn's character is named Andres Bonifacio. The
casualness of naming such a character after a major revolutionary leader, albeit one who never fought the Americans,
is remarkable.

And yet, oddly, the war remained to be rediscovered as a
nationalist totem. The decade of the 1890s, in which the
Filipinos fought and won and lost several revolutions,
against both the Spanish and the Americans, provided ten
years of universal national experiences for the islands. Although different in specifics, every region had its war stories
from that period, its victories and losses. The Philippine-

American War was part of a Filipino experience, one that had the potential to bring a national vision to an archipelago full of people of different races, creeds, religions, cultures, and languages. There was a nascent nationalism in that experience, one waiting for the right moment to flower.

The Americans assisted in the creation of a Filipino nationalism as well, by training a large number of Filipinos in the English language. English essentially became the national tongue, and the colonial government created a system of education that raised literacy rates to over 50 percent in 1941 (up from 20 percent in 1901).[3] The practical utility of that was obvious: by imposing a language that spanned the archipelago, the Americans facilitated trade and governance. But a common language brought with it cultural unification, and created a class of Filipinos—civil servants, merchants, and others—who thought of themselves as Filipino first and Tagalog or Moro second. Interestingly, Aguinaldo himself steadfastly refused to learn English, perhaps sensing that his Philippines were being rewritten by the new idiom.[4] Any nation is, of course, imagined, and the United States facilitated the creation of that construct by building economic, social, and linguistic ties among the islands.[5]

The teasing ambiguity thus remains. America helped the Philippines become a nation, by violence and education: blood and words. Nowhere is that clearer than in the last years of World War II, when the signal of the Philippines' liberation from yet another conqueror was the striding ashore of Gen. Douglas MacArthur, "returning," as he had promised. That the son of Arthur MacArthur, the man responsible for the final breaking of Aguinaldo's Philippine

Republic and the insurgency it fostered, was seen decades later as a symbol of Filipino deliverance is astonishing. In a sense, it completed the journey started in the 1890s. At one end of that journey was Arthur; at the other was Douglas. The independence that almost immediately followed MacArthur's wade ashore simply confirmed the journey and the arrival of the Philippines as a nation in the Western sense.

America as a World Power

The Philippine-American War did not affect only the Philippines. For the United States, it—even more than the Spanish-American War—was the concrete assertion of a global American reach. After the Philippine-American War, the United States was, like it or not, a critical actor in the world's affairs. These first steps onto the broader world stage did not escape the notice of other powers. There was a general sense that the United States was taking its proper place among the Western powers. It was an era of small wars and colonial uprisings. The Philippine-American War could be compared to the Boer War in South Africa between the British and Afrikaner farmers (1899–1902), and Samar could be paralleled with the Congo, where the Belgian king treated his colony with such genocidal ferocity that he outraged even the normally complacent Europeans and inspired Joseph Conrad to write *Heart of Darkness*. The world was being split down to its last parcel among the Western powers, and the Philippines were one more chunk to be absorbed.

But a particular point remains critical. The United States had been an Atlantic power already. The consolidation of U.S. control over the West Coast and the lands in between and the acquisition of the Philippines demanded that the United States commit to becoming a Pacific power as well. The archipelago gave the United States a foothold in Asia, close by to the rising power of Japan and the voluminous markets of China. But it was an outpost a long distance from continental America. Such an outpost demanded a substantial defensive effort to protect it.

It quickly became clear that the defensive effort required was simply not sustainable. The Philippines were impossible to defend without the commitment of resources at a level that the United States was not willing to make. As the strategic analyst Robert Johnson would say in 1915:

> The taking of the Philippines from Spain may be ranked among the worst military blunders committed by any American government—it is difficult to put the matter more strongly. It is a weak, ex-centric military position, fundamentally indefensible against any strong transpacific power, but inevitably a magnet to draw troops and ships away from our shores.[6]

It took only twenty-six years for Johnson's words to be proven deeply prophetic. The ease with which Japanese forces in 1941–42 overwhelmed the American defenses makes Spanish efforts in 1898 look a bit better. The critical difference, of course, was that the Americans were able to rebuild and return in a way that the Spanish never did.

Philippine independence after the war was over was thus not merely a recognition of the new Philippine nation. It was also a sensible strategic move. The new configuration, in which the United States held on to such outposts as the naval base at Subic Bay, resembled one of the options that

McKinley had considered in the aftermath of the victory over Spain. The Philippines in the Cold War were independent, but something of a protectorate of the United States, and the reach provided by American bases there enabled the United States to maintain its authority in the Pacific without the drain of resources that defending the islands would have required. That reach allowed the United States to protect Taiwan and to intervene in Korea and Vietnam, supplying and sustaining large land and naval forces.

Strangely, the reach that allowed the United States to wage war and lose in Vietnam brought the Philippine-American War back to historical consciousness. The history of 1899–1902 had been treated in a number of works in the immediate aftermath, but it had largely faded from American view in the 1920s, 1930s, and 1940s, lost in the shadow of the conventional wars of 1914–18 and 1939–45. It never emerged from those shadows, but the United States instead followed it into the darkness during the guerrilla war in Vietnam. Suddenly Americans were again fighting a war of outpost, patrol, and ambush, and unlike in the Philippines, losing that war. Counterinsurgency there roused interest in earlier counterinsurgencies. Atrocities there roused interest in earlier atrocities.

But the reasons for interest sometimes overwhelmed good history, and shaped the conflict from 1899 to 1902 in ways that obscured rather than explained what happened in those three years. The war became wholly one of guerrilla fighting and atrocities, an oversimplified fin de siècle Vietnam, useful primarily for mining lessons for future such conflicts. Lost was the rich complexity of the real war.

That was a grievous loss, for the convoluted density of the Philippine-American War remains a historical phenomenon in its own right. It was a revolution before all, as Filipino groups sought to fight off the imperial masters who had ruled them, if somnolently at times, for nearly four hundred years. That revolution, we should not forget, was ultimately a Filipino victory. The assistance given by Dewey at Manila Bay was small enough, as such assistance goes. It was the Army of Liberation that overwhelmed Spanish resistance in most of the islands and the Army of Liberation that would likely, although probably with heavier casualties, have overwhelmed Spanish resistance in the city of Manila itself. What we might call the Philippine Rebellion came to an end in August of 1898, when the last major center of Spanish resistance in the islands surrendered.

That that surrender was to an American force should not obscure the depth of the Filipino victory. The Army of Liberation had defeated the Spanish. But, of course, the conflict was not over. The American decision to take the islands made further conflict inevitable. The choice, fueled by the old long-standing sense of manifest destiny that had pushed American settlers, society, and government westward through the nineteenth century and by a new manifest destiny that saw the United States as too powerful to confine itself to one continent or hemisphere, started what would best be labeled the First Philippine-American War. Despite arguments by people at the time, as well as later historians, this was classically a war, and remarkably unlike an insurgency. The two sides were both states substantially sovereign, using conventional armies, fighting conventional battles, with conventional lines and weapons. The conflict of 1899 simply was not a guerrilla war; it was as conventional a conflict between two legitimate states as was any other American war of the nineteenth century and more so than some.

That the U.S. Army overwhelmed the Filipino Army of Liberation in relatively short order does not change this fact. Overwhelm it it did, in a series of effectively planned, supplied, and contested campaigns in the spring and fall of 1899. The credit on the American side for the successful execution lies at all levels of the army. Otis put together ambitious plans, his subordinates carried them out, sometimes with great difficulty, and the ordinary soldiers fought with both bravery and intelligence. Most impressively, the American officers and enlisted men learned the early lessons quickly and used them to great effect. For an army still loaded with Civil War veterans, whose memories of that war told them firmly that frontal assaults against entrenched positions were organized suicide, to learn as fast as it did that frontal assaults against entrenched positions were in fact likely to be successful against the soldiers of the Army of Liberation demonstrates a remarkable tactical flexibility. That flexibility won the war.

On the Filipino side, blame for the loss can accrue at all levels, as well. Aguinaldo certainly demonstrated little that resembled military genius. His officers often seemed more concerned with advancing their own causes than the causes of the army or the republic. The ordinary Filipino soldiers frequently fought with great resolution, but many times they did not, and even that resolution was often not matched by skill. There are reasonable explanations for all these things, but the fact remained that a Filipino army that had done well against the Spanish could not sustain the effort against the Americans.

The desperate realization of that fact led Aguinaldo to turn to guerrilla tactics. He has been criticized for not doing so earlier, but we should recognize that by so doing he was essentially abdicating the sovereignty of the Philippine Republic. Guerrilla war gains anonymity for its users, but it sacrifices all territory and public government. The Philippine Republic went underground when the war did, never to see the light of day again.

It is hard to say that the guerrilla war—which truly was an insurgency—went any better for the Filipinos. Certainly, it extended the conflict. But there were only a few moments in which it appeared as if Aguinaldo's forces could truly inflict such heavy casualties on U.S. forces as to compel them to leave. The fall of 1900 was one such time, and if William Jennings Bryan had won the presidency in November of that year, there is some chance that the United States would have withdrawn.

But other than this, while the guerrilla campaign was somewhat more effective than the conventional one, in the end the result was the same. By the fall of 1901, with Aguinaldo imprisoned, other political leaders exiled to Guam, and the surrenders of many of the remaining rebel leaders, the campaign was winding down. The catastrophic American response on Samar seems more like frustration expressed as brutality than a reasoned military response. It was a bitter coda to what had been, by the standards of counterinsurgency or, for that matter, late-nineteenth-century colonial wars, a relatively moderate conflict.

Both sides committed atrocities, some large and some small, but for the most part the war was executed without the kind of wholesale slaughter that was all too common in that period. One of the few exceptions to this were the ravages of cholera in 1902. Despite the fact that cholera outbreaks had occurred at regular intervals in Philippine history, the United States must shoulder a substantial portion of the blame. The concentration policy was an effective one militarily, but it helped create sanitary conditions that, once the weather eased, inexorably led to an epidemic. Hundreds of thousands died as a result.

We should not overestimate either of those factors, though. Had the war truly been universally vicious, it seems deeply unlikely that the Filipinos would have reconciled themselves to the Americans so quickly and, even after independence, found themselves in an affectionate relationship with their erstwhile overlord. The forgetting of the war that Reynaldo Ileto pointed to is the clearest evidence that neither Samar nor the cholera epidemic were typical.

In the end, it was a war of crossroads for all involved. For the Spanish, it was, along with the war in Cuba, the end of an empire long past its days of glory. For the Americans, it was the final war of a frontier ethos that had driven them across a continent and the first war of a global ethos that would send them out over the oceans. For the Filipinos, it was a defeat that looked, in later decades, a lot like victory. A collection of islands, fractured by culture and society, became, largely because of the shared experience of revolution, war, and insurgency, a self-conceived nation. They had reached for independence and found, for a brief moment then and longer later, something that looked more like sovereignty.

Further Reading

Distressingly enough, the literature on the Philippine-American War is not of particularly high quality, with a number of important exceptions. The war itself has long been neglected, and those who have turned to it have tended to do so to promote their own agendas. Those agendas sometimes led to history that was more interesting for what it said about the author and the author's era than about 1899–1902.

Immediately after the war, most of the works celebrated the civilizing influence of the American presence. There were some anti-imperialist works as a counterweight, but for the most part America's role in the Philippines was one of progress. The Philippine-American War largely disappeared as a topic of much study in the 1930s and '40s.

Philippine-American relations were relaxed and amicable and—the prevailing attitude seemed—nothing should disturb that, certainly not the minor unpleasantness of 1899–1902. The start of World War II in 1941 pushed the conflict further out of historical consciousness, an exile that continued into the postwar years.

The war only reappeared in the 1960s as a stand-in for a current conflict. Historians looking aghast at the war in Vietnam discovered suddenly that America had fought another such war in Southeast Asia more than sixty years previously. That earlier war, they thought, could be mined for lessons for the current war, or simply to illustrate the appalling nature of all such guerrilla campaigns. Unfortunately the history this produced focused to the exclusion of almost all else on the malevolence and futility of the American effort. One practical effect of this was to overestimate the importance of the last year of the war. Another effect was the dawning surprise of the historians at the fact that—unlike in Vietnam—the United States actually managed to *win* in the Philippines. The contorted hand waving necessary to deal with the victory often produced a breeze that might have cooled American and Filipino tempers alike in that hot Manila summer of 1898. The two wars in Southeast Asia seemed linked as tragedy and farce, and the history that this vision produced was not of the highest grade.

A concurrent historiography developed in the Philippines, which reimposed a national vision on what had been a fragmented archipelago. Searching for an event to use as the founding date for Filipino nationalism, Filipino scholars found the war, and liked it. The sleepiness of the last several centuries of Spanish rule provided little in the way of inspiration. But the decade and a half after José Rizal's

1889 visit to the Wild West show in Paris was stirring and martial and seemingly Filipino. There, the nation could be born. The Philippine-American War thus became, in retrospect, a national revolution. This made for stirring tales, but, unfortunately, rarely for sober history. The result has been a cascade of solid local studies but few good large-scale accounts of the war.

Only in the late 1980s did a set of serious scholars emerge who would reexamine the war in the Philippines carefully and with diligent scholarship. The work they have produced over the last two decades has begun the process of reclaiming the Philippines from ideology and is well worth reading. But the lesson remains: one should pick carefully when exploring the era and the war. What follows are my recommendations of particularly useful or interesting works, and those topics that I found particularly interesting. Thus, the recommendations are more eclectic than categorical.

Perhaps the best place to start is with Brian Linn's foundational work on the Philippine conflict, *The Philippine War, 1899–1902* (Lawrence: University Press of Kansas, 2000). His earlier *The U.S. Army and Counterinsurgency in the Philippine War, 1899–1902* (Chapel Hill: University of North Carolina Press, 1989) is also valuable but more focused on the American army's experience. An earlier work by John Gates, *Schoolboys and Krags: The United States Army in the Philippines, 1898–1902* (Westport, Conn.: Greenwood, 1973), serves as a useful corrective to the "Philippines as Vietnam" school.

No exploration of the history of the Philippines would be complete without reading something by Renato Constantino, the noted Filipino scholar. In this context, Renato

Constantino and Letizia R. Constantino, *The Philippines: A Past Revisited* (Quezon City, Philippines: Tala Publishing Services, 1975), would be the best place to start. It should be noted that Constantino is sometimes more interested in the war as a national event than in the war as it really was. Finally, there is always the daunting prospect of John R.M. Taylor, *The Philippine Insurrection against the United States*, 5 vols. (Pasay City, Philippines: Eugenio Lopez Foundation, 1971). This work, all five volumes of it, is a remarkable accomplishment that combines history and documentation. Taylor, a U.S. Army officer who had served in the Philippines, was tasked with writing the official history. He did so, using thousands of intercepted insurgent messages, but the project, because of bureaucratic infighting, was not published until nearly seventy years later by a press in the Philippines.

There are specific topics within the larger war that are worthy of further exploration. The reaction of African-Americans, both civilians and soldiers, to the Philippine conflict is admirably handled in William B. Gatewood, Jr., *Black Americans and the White Man's Burden* (Urbana: University of Illinois Press, 1975). His follow-up volume, William Gatewood, Jr., *"Smoked Yankees" and the Struggle for Empire: Letters from Negro Soldiers, 1898–1902* (Fayetteville: University of Arkansas Press, 1987), provides the raw letters of African-American soldiers writing home. The day-to-day specifics of the military campaign on both sides also make for a choice subject. Unfortunately, the Filipino side has not been graced yet with a work that looks at the nuts and bolts of the Army of Liberation's conventional campaigns against the Spanish and Americans and the guerrilla campaign against the United States. On the American side, for the battle of Manila, I do not think that Karl Irving Faust, *Campaigning in the Philippines* (San Francisco: Hicks-Judd, 1899), has been matched. William Thaddeus Sexton, *Soldiers in the Sun* (Harrisburg, Pa.: Military Publishing Company, 1939), is good for the whole war. On the Philippine side of things, there are a range of fascinating works. Glenn Anthony May's *Inventing a Hero* (New York: University of Wisconsin Press, 1996) is an exploration of the situation before the United States arrived and the mythmaking that has grown up around that period and the figure of Andres Bonifacio. May's earlier work, *The Battle for Batangas: a Philippine Province at War* (New Haven: Yale University Press, 1991), is also useful. A similar study of the experience of a province during the war is Resil B. Morales, *The War Against the Americans: Resistance and Collaboration in Cebu: 1899–1906* (Manila: Ateneo de Manila University Press, 1999). Also interesting, albeit highly defensive, is Aguinaldo's work: Emilio Aguinaldo and Vicente Albano Pacis, *A Second Look at America* (New York: Robert Speller & Sons, 1957). His later memoirs offer a similar level of special pleading, at greater length.

For a sense of the larger world that gave the conflict its context, a number of works are good: Walter LaFeber, *The American Age: United States Foreign Policy at Home and Abroad since 1750* (New York: Norton, 1989), offers a concise view of the foreign policy situation that confronted McKinley and Roosevelt. David Traxel's *1898* (New York: Knopf, 1998) focuses on that year but is still valuable for before and after. Eric Rauchway's *Murdering McKinley: The Making of Theodore Roosevelt's America* (New York: Hill and Wang, 2003) is an excellent introduction to the domestic scene. Joel H. Silbey's *The American Political Nation,*

1838–1893 (Stanford, Calif.: Stanford University Press,
1991) guides the reader through the evolution of the American political systems of the nineteenth century. Ronald
Spector's biography of Admiral Dewey is well written and
useful: Ronald Spector, *Admiral of the New Empire: The Life
and Career of George Dewey* (Baton Rouge: Louisiana State
University Press, 1974). To understand the U.S. Navy at
the turn of the century, see Harold Sprout, *The Rise of
American Naval Power, 1776–1918* (Princeton: Princeton
University Press, 1939, 1967). Finally, two works by Edward Coffman explain the U.S. Army of the era perhaps
better than anything else: Edward M. Coffman, *The Old
Army: A Portrait of the American Army in Peacetime, 1784–
1898* (New York: Oxford University Press, 1986); and Edward M. Coffman, *The Regulars: The American Army,
1898–1941* (Cambridge, Mass.: Harvard University Press,
2004).

Notes

Introduction: The Urgency of the Asking

1. Resil B. Morales, *The War Against the Americans: Resistance and Collaboration in Cebu: 1899–1906* (Manila: Ateneo de Manila University Press, 1999), 1.
2. Renato Constantino, *Neocolonial Identity and Counter-Consciousness* (White Plains, N.Y.: M.E. Sharpe, 1978), 261. See also, for a similar American view, John M. Gates, *The United States Army and Irregular Warfare*, self-published on the Internet at http://www.wooster.edu/history/jgates/book-contents.html, 11.
3. Brian Linn, *The Philippine War, 1899–1902* (Lawrence: University Press of Kansas, 2000).
4. John Larkin, "Philippine History Reconsidered: A Socioeconomic Perspective," *American Historical Review* 87, no. 3 (June 1982): 595–628.

1. A War of Frontier and Empire

1. The account of the meeting appears in a diary kept by Simeon Villa. Captured and translated by the American military, it offers a useful insight into Aguinaldo's thoughts in late 1899. Obviously, the translation may not be perfectly reliable. It is, nonetheless, the best we have. See John R.M. Taylor, *The Philippine Insurrection against the United States*, vol. 5 (Pasay City, Philippines: Eugenio Lopez Foundation, 1971), 7–10.

2. Edgar Wickberg, *The Chinese in Philippine Life* (New Haven: Yale University Press, 1965), 4.

3. Benedict Anderson, *The Spectre of Comparisons: Nationalism, Southeast Asia, and the World* (London: Verso, 1998), 195.

4. John Leddy Phelan, "Free Versus Compulsory Labor: Mexico and the Philippines 1540–1648," *Comparative Studies in Society and History* 1, no. 2 (January 1959): 189–201.

5. John Larkin, "Philippine History Reconsidered: A Socioeconomic Perspective," *American Historical Review* 87, no. 3 (June 1982): 613.

6. Ibid., 616.

7. Peter C. Smith, "Crisis Mortality in the Nineteenth Century Philippines: Data from Parish Records," *Journal of Asian Studies* 38, no. 1 (November 1978): 51–76.

8. Glenn May, "150,000 Missing Filipinos: A Demographic Crisis in Batangas, 1887–1903," *Annales de Démographie Historique* 21 (1985): 215–43, 216–18.

9. David Barrows, "The Governor-General of the Philippines under Spain and the United States," *American Historical Review* 21, no. 2 (1916): 288–311.

10. Quoted in Sharon Delmendo, *The Star-Entangled Banner: One Hundred Years of America in the Philippines* (New Brunswick, N.J.: Rutgers University Press, 2004), 27.

11. Robert Asprey, *War in the Shadows: The Guerilla in History* (New York: Morrow, 1994 [1976]), 122; Delmendo, *Star-Entangled Banner*, 21–46.

12. For an analysis of one particular set of ethnic suspicions see David Porter, *Ilokos: A Non-Tagalog Response to Social, Political, and Economic Change, 1870–1910* (Ithaca, N.Y.: Cornell University Press, 1980).

13. Asprey, *War in the Shadows*, 123.

14. Renato Constantino, *Neocolonial Identity and Counter-Consciousness* (White Plains, N.Y.: M.E. Sharpe, 1978), 270.

15. Renato Constantino, *A History of the Philippines: From the Spanish Colonization to the Second World War* (New York: Monthly Review Press, 1975), 190.

16. Quoted in William Thaddeus Sexton, *Soldiers in the Sun* (Harrisburg, Pa.: Military Publishing Company, 1939), 27.

17. Quote and statistics in Edward Coffman, *The Old Army: A Portrait of the American Army in Peacetime, 1784–1898* (Oxford, U.K.: Oxford University Press, 1986), 215.

18. Ibid., 263.

19. Dodge quote in ibid., 329. Marshall quote in Larry Bland, ed., *George C. Marshall Interviews and Reminiscences for Forrest C. Pogue* (Lexington, Va.: George C. Marshall Foundation, 1996), 130.

20. Quoted in Coffman, *The Old Army,* 231.

21. Quoted in ibid., 230.

22. Quoted in ibid., 284.

23. Brian McAllister Linn, "The Long Twilight of the Frontier Army," *Western Historical Quarterly* 27, no. 2 (summer 1996): 141–67.

24. Quoted in Kenneth Hagan, *This People's Navy: The Making of American Sea Power* (New York: Free Press, 1991), 178.

25. Roosevelt to Mahan, May 12, 1890, in H. W. Brands, ed., *The Selected Letters of Theodore Roosevelt* (New York: Cooper Square Press, 2001), 72.

26. Benjamin Harrison, *Public Papers and Addresses of Benjamin Harrison, March 4, 1889–March 4, 1893* (Washington, D.C.: Government Printing Office, 1893), 32.

27. Quoted in Hagan, *This People's Navy,* 195.

28. Harold Sprout, *The Rise of American Naval Power, 1776–1918* (Princeton: Princeton University Press, 1967 [1939]), 215.

29. Harrison, *Public Papers and Addresses of Benjamin Harrison,* 114.

30. Richard Welch, Jr., *The Presidencies of Grover Cleveland* (Kansas City: University Press of Kansas, 1988), 173–74.

2. McKinley and American Imperialism

1. Harry Sievers, ed., *William McKinley, 1843–1901: Chronology, Documents, Bibliographical Aids* (Dobbs Ferry, N.Y.: Oceana Publications, 1970), 24.

2. David Trask, *1898* (New York: Knopf, 1998), 90.
3. "Directive from the State Department to Stewart Lyndon Woodford," July 16, 1897, quoted in Sievers, ed., *William McKinley*, 30–31.
4. McKinley's State of the Union Address, December 6, 1897, in Sievers, ed., *William McKinley*, 30–31.
5. Hearst quote in Trask, *1898*, 108; Dawes quote, entry for March 28, 1898, Charles Dawes, *A Journal of the McKinley Years* (Chicago: Lakeside Press, 1950), 150; newspaper quote from the *Sacramento Evening Bee*, March 11, 1898, quoted in Julius Pratt, "American Business and the Spanish-American War," *Hispanic American Historical Review* 14, no. 2 (May 1934): 163–201.
6. "Submarine mine" from McKinley, "Special Message to Congress," March 28, 1898, in Sievers, ed., *William McKinley*, 30–31. Dawes quote from Dawes, *Journal of the McKinley Years*, 153.
7. Louis Stanley Young, *The Life and Heroic Deeds of Admiral Dewey* (Philadelphia: Globe Bible Publishing Company, 1899), 55.
8. Quoted in Trask, *1898*, 111.
9. Richard Hofstadter, "Manifest Destiny and the Philippines," in *The Paranoid Style in American Politics* (Cambridge, Mass.: Harvard University Press, 1996 [1965]), 173–200, 195.
10. Emilio Aguinaldo and Vicente Albano Pacis, *A Second Look at America* (New York: Robert Speller & Sons, 1957), 19.
11. Walter LaFeber, *The American Age: United States Foreign Policy at Home and Abroad since 1750* (New York: Norton, 1989), 193.
12. John McCutcheon, diary entry for April 1898, in A. B. Feuer, ed., *America at War: The Philippines, 1898–1913* (Westport, Conn.: Praeger, 2002), 3.
13. Quoted in Kenneth Hagan, *This People's Navy: The Making of American Sea Power* (New York: Free Press, 1991), 219.
14. McCutcheon, diary entry for May 1, 1898, in Feuer, ed., *America at War*, 19.
15. Quoted in Hofstadter, "Manifest Destiny and the Philippines," 173–200, 193.
16. Quoted in Young, *Heroic Deeds*, 111.
17. For cigarettes, see Hagan, *This People's Navy*, 220; for statues, see William McElwee, *The Art of War from Waterloo to Mons* (London: Weidenfeld and Nicolson, 1974), 277; for quote, see Young, *Heroic Deeds*, v.

18. Aguinaldo's side of things can be found in Aguinaldo and Pacis, *A Second Look at America*, 36–39.
19. Ibid., 70–71.
20. Proclamation, June 23, 1898, in John R.M. Taylor, *The Philippine Insurrection against the United States; A Compilation of Documents with Notes and Introduction* (Pasay City, Philippines: Eugenio Lopez Foundation, 1971), 31.
21. Edward Coffman, *The Hilt of the Sword: The Career of Peyton C. March* (Madison: University of Wisconsin Press, 1966), 13.
22. William Thaddeus Sexton, *Soldiers in the Sun* (Harrisburg, Pa.: Military Publishing Company, 1939), 24.
23. Diary entry for June 27, 1898, Theodore Wurm Papers, Military History Institute, Carlisle, Pa.
24. Quoted in Sexton, *Soldiers in the Sun*, 20.
25. Smell and coffee from Sexton, *Soldiers in the Sun*, 20, 31. Christner quote from R. Jay Gift, *Attitudes of the State Volunteer Soldiers Who Fought in the Philippines during the Spanish-American War and the Philippine Insurrection* (Shippensburg, Pa.: Shippensburg State College, 1976), no page number.
26. Quoted in Sexton, *Soldiers in the Sun*, 32.
27. Quoted in David Joel Steinberg, "An Ambiguous Legacy: Years at War in the Philippines," *Public Affairs* 45, no. 2 (summer 1972): 168.
28. Quoted in Grania Bolton, "Military Diplomacy and National Liberation: Insurgent-American Relations After the Fall of Manila," *Military Affairs* 36, no. 3 (October 1972): 99–104.
29. Diary entry for August 1, 1898, Theodore Wurm Papers.
30. Oscar Davis quoted in Coffman, *The Hilt of the Sword*, 16.
31. Diary entry for August 16, 1898, Theodore Wurm Papers.
32. Quoted in Lewis O. Saum, "The Western Volunteer and 'The New Empire,'" *Pacific Northwest Quarterly* 57, no. 1 (January 1996): 18–27.
33. Hofstadter, "Manifest Destiny and the Philippines," 173–200, 187.
34. Julie A. Tuason, "The Ideology of Empire in *National Geographic's* Coverage of the Philippines, 1898–1908," *Geographical Review* 89, no. 1 (January 1999): 34–53.
35. Joel H. Silbey, *Storm over Texas: The Annexation Controversy and the Road to the Civil War* (Oxford, U.K.: Oxford University Press, 2005), 80–90.

36. Mayan to John S. Barnes, July 21, 1898, in Robert Seager and Doris D. Maguire, *Letters and Papers of Alfred Thayer Mahan, Volume II, 1890–1901* (Annapolis, Md.: Naval Institute Press, 1975), 566.

37. Dawes, *Journal of the McKinley Years*, 166.

38. Young, *Heroic Deeds*, 94. Also Thomas A. Bailey, "Dewey and the Germans at Manila Bay," *American Historical Review* 45, no. 1 (October 1939): 59–81; Alfred Vagts, "Hopes and Fears of an American-German War, 1870–1915," *Political Science Quarterly* 54, no. 4 (December 1939): 514–35.

39. James K. Eyre, Jr., "Russia and the American Acquisition of the Philippines," *Mississippi Valley Historical Review* 28, no. 4 (March 1942): 539–62.

40. Seager and Maguire, *Letters and Papers of Alfred Thayer Mahan*, 2:582.

41. William R. Braisted, "The Philippine Naval Base Problem," *Mississippi Valley Historical Review* 41, no. 1 (June 1954): 21–40.

42. Daniel Schirmer, *The Philippines Reader: A History of Colonialism, Neocolonialism, Dictatorship, and Resistance* (Boston: South End Press, 1987), 21.

43. Robert Rydell, "The Trans-Mississippi and International Exposition: 'To Work Out the Problem of International Civilization,' " *American Quarterly* 33, no. 5 (winter 1981): 587–607, 603–604.

44. Lewis L. Gould, *The Spanish-American War and President McKinley* (Lawrence: University Press of Kansas, 1982), 109.

45. Whitelaw Reid to C. Inman Barnard, July 23, 1898, in David R. Conosta and Jessica R. Hawthorne, eds., "Rise to World Power: Selected Letters of Whitelaw Reid, 1895–1912," *Transactions of the American Philosophical Society* 76, no. 2 (1986): 141.

46. Whitelaw Reid to Donald Nicholson, August 8, 1898, in ibid., 43; Reid to McKinley, October 4, 1898, in ibid.

47. Henry Cabot Lodge to Henry White, August 12, 1898, quoted in Brian Damiani, *Advocates of Empire: William McKinley, the Senate, and American Expansion, 1898–1899* (New York: Garland, 1987), 39.

48. Damiani, *Advocates of Empire*, 98.

49. Whitelaw Reid to McKinley, October 4, 1898, in Conosta and Hawthorne, eds., "Rise to World Power," 45.

50. For great power attitudes, see Eyre, "Russia and the American Acquisition of the Philippines," 539–62; for "little dog," see

Whitelaw Reid to John Hay, October 26, 1898, in Conosta and Hawthorne, eds., "Rise to World Power," 47.

51. Diary entry for August 18, 1898, Theodore Wurm Papers.

52. Unnamed soldier, December 24, 1898, quoted in *Facts about the Filipinos* 1, no. 6 (July 15, 1901): 6.

53. Quoted in Jerry Cooper, *Citizens as Soldiers: A History of the North Dakota National Guard* (Lincoln: University of Nebraska Press, 2005), 64.

54. Gift, *Attitudes of the State Volunteer Soldiers*, no page number.

55. Public statement, January 5, 1899, in Taylor, *The Philippine Insurrection*, 52–53.

56. David Sturtevant, *Agrarian Unrest in the Philippines* (Ames, Ohio: Center for International Studies, Ohio University, 1969), 8.

57. Quoted in Cooper, *Citizens as Soldiers*, 67.

58. "Daily Report," in *Facts about the Filipinos* 1, no. 5 (May 1901): 59.

59. Ibid., 60.

60. Quoted in Gift, *Attitudes of the State Volunteer Soldiers*, no page number.

3. "At the Cannon's Mouth"

1. Lewis O. Saum, "The Western Volunteer and 'The New Empire,' " *Pacific Northwest Quarterly* 57, no. 1 (January 1996): 18–27, 23.

2. Karl Irving Faust, *Campaigning in the Philippines* (San Francisco: Hicks-Judd, 1899), 136.

3. Diary entry for March 4, 1899, Theodore Wurm Papers, Military History Institute, Carlisle, Pa.

4. William Richard Gordon, *History of the 10th Pennsylvania Volunteer Infantry* (Pennsylvania), 70–72.

5. Figures and quote from David F. Trask, *The War with Spain in 1898* (New York: Macmillan, 1981), 245.

6. John Taylor, ed., *Compilation of Philippine Insurgent Records: Telegraphic Correspondence of Emilio Aguinaldo, July 15, 1898 to February 28, 1899* (Washington, D.C.: Government Printing Office, 1903), no page number but chronological at September 13, 1898.

7. David A. Armstrong, *Bullets and Bureaucrats: The Machine Gun and the United States Army, 1861–1916* (Westport, Conn.: Greenwood, 1982), 115.

8. Russell Gilmore, " 'The New Courage': Rifles and Soldier Individualism, 1876–1918," *Military Affairs* 40, no. 3 (October 1976): 97–102.

9. Roger Pauly, *Firearms: The Life Story of a Technology* (Westport, Conn.: Greenwood, 2004), 115–16.

10. Quoted in Jerry Cooper, *Citizens as Soldiers: A History of the North Dakota National Guard* (Lincoln: University of Nebraska Press, 2005), 81.

11. Quoted in A. B. Feuer, ed., *America at War: The Philippines, 1898–1913* (Westport, Conn.: Praeger, 2002), 89.

12. Alexander Hawkins, "Official History of the Operations of the 10th Pennsylvania Infantry, U.S.V. in the Campaign in the Philippine Islands," in Karl Irving Faust, *Campaigning in the Philippines* (New York: Arno, 1970), 15.

13. Ibid.

14. Herbert M. Reddy, U.S. Infantry, 6th Regiment, "Ridin' Herd in the Philippines," 2, Spanish-American War Survey, Military History Institute, Carlisle, Pa.

15. "Annual Report of Major-General E. S. Otis, U.S.V., Commanding Department of the Pacific and Eighth Army Corps, Military Governor in the Philippine Islands," in *The Annual Report of the War Department for the Fiscal Year Ended June 30, 1899*, vol. 1, part 4 (Washington, D.C.: Government Printing Office, 1899), 100.

16. Ibid.

17. James H. Blount, *The American Occupation of the Philippines, 1898–1912* (New York: Putnam, 1912), 196.

18. John R.M. Taylor, *The Philippine Insurrection against the United States* (Pasay City, Philippines: Eugenio Lopez Foundation, 1971), vol. 5, 609.

19. Arthur MacArthur, "Report of Field Operations of the Second Division, Eighth Army Corps, for March–May, 1899," in *The Annual Report of the War Department for the Fiscal Year Ended June 30, 1899*, vol. 1, part 5 (Washington, D.C.: Government Printing Office, 1899), 382.

20. Quoted in ibid., 385.

21. Ibid., 391–92.

22. Ibid., 393.

23. Ibid., 395.

24. Don Russell, *Campaigning with King: Charles King, Chronicler of*

the Old Army, edited by Paul Hedren (Lincoln: University of Nebraska Press, 1991), 125.

25. Quoted in Feuer, ed., *America at War,* 140.

26. Quoted in Garel Grunder, *The Philippines and the United States* (Norman: University of Oklahoma Press, 1951), 40.

27. August 26, 1898, quoted in William B. Gatewood, Jr., *Black Americans and the White Man's Burden* (Urbana: University of Illinois Press, 1975), 187.

28. Mark Joseph Peceny, *The Promotion of Democracy in U.S. Policy during Military Interventions* (Ph.D. dissertation, Stanford University, 1992), 76-78.

29. Fred H. Harrington, "The Anti-Imperialist Movement in the United States, 1898-1900," *Mississippi Valley Historical Review* 22, no. 2 (September 1935): 211-30.

30. Quoted in Grunder, *The Philippines and the United States,* 42-43.

31. Walter L. Williams, "United States Indian Policy and the Debate over Philippine Annexation: Implications for the Origins of American Imperialism," *Journal of American History* 66, no. 4 (March 1980): 810-31.

32. John W. Burgess, "How May the United States Govern its Extra-Continental Territory?," *Political Science Quarterly* 14, no. 1 (March 1899): 1-18; Williams, "United States Indian Policy and the Debate over Philippine Annexation," 810-31. Despite these seemingly settled precedents, the legal discussion over the "Insular Territories" acquired in 1898—Puerto Rico, Guam, and the Philippines—continued. See Lanny Thompson, "The Imperial Republic: A Comparison of the Insular Territories under U.S. Dominion after 1898," *Pacific Historical Review* 71, no. 4 (November 2002): 535-74.

33. Quoted in Gatewood, *Black Americans,* 183.

34. Quoted in Peceny, *Promotion of Democracy,* 109.

35. Grunder, *The Philippines and the United States,* 47.

36. Quoted in Peceny, *Promotion of Democracy,* 113.

37. Charles Dawes, *A Journal of the McKinley Years* (Chicago: Lakeside Press, 1950), 183.

38. David Axeen, " 'Heroes of the Engine Room': American 'Civilization' and the War with Spain," *American Quarterly* 36, no. 4 (autumn 1984): 481-502, 496.

39. Dean C. Worcester, June 1898, quoted in Julie A. Tuason, "The Ideology of Empire in *National Geographic's* Coverage of the

Philippines, 1898–1908," *Geographical Review* 89, no. 1 (January 1999): 34–53.

40. Gordon, *History of the 10th Pennsylvania Volunteer Infantry*, 80.
41. Quoted in Forrest Pogue, *George C. Marshall: Education of a General, 1880–1939* (New York: Viking, 1963), 52.
42. Tuason, "The Ideology of Empire," 34–53.
43. Quoted in David Joel Steinberg, "An Ambiguous Legacy: Years at War in the Philippines," *Public Affairs* 45, no. 2 (summer 1972): 168.
44. Timothy Deady, "Lessons from a Successful Counterinsurgency: The Philippines, 1899–1902," *Parameters* 35, no. 1 (spring 2005): 57.
45. John R.M. Taylor, *The Philippine Insurrection against the United States: A Compilation of Documents with Notes and Introduction*, vol. 4 (Pasay City, Philippines: Eugenio Lopez Foundation, 1971), 544.
46. Ibid., 576.
47. "General Orders to the Commanders of Zone Operations and Provincial Military Commanders," February 7, 1899, in Taylor, *Philippine Insurrection*, 3.
48. Severino de las Alas, "Circular to the Provincial Chiefs of This Archipelago Regarding the Cause of the Death of General Antonio Luna and His Aide, Colonel Francisco Roman," in Taylor, *Philippine Insurrection*, 657.
49. For example, Deady, "Lessons from a Successful Counterinsurgency," 11.

4. A New Army Arrives

1. Wilmer Blackett, Army Service Experience Questionnaire, Spanish-American War Survey Box 228, Military History Institute, Carlisle, Pa.
2. Quotes from John D. LaWall, Company I, 27th Regiment, U.S. Volunteers, "Sixteen Months in the Philippines," Military History Institute, Carlisle, Pa.
3. Ibid.
4. Ibid.
5. Russell Roth, *Muddy Glory: America's "Indian Wars" in the Phil-*

ippines (W. Hanover, Mass.: Christopher Publishing House, 1981), 60.

6. William B. Gatewood, Jr., *Black Americans and the White Man's Burden* (Urbana: University of Illinois Press, 1975), 3.

7. Unnamed African-American woman from Minnesota, quoted in ibid., 223.

8. Information and quotes from ibid., 182, 185, 190.

9. Ibid., 199.

10. Ibid., 192, 194.

11. Harry Smith of the *Cleveland Gazette*, April 22, 1899, quoted in ibid., 202.

12. Unnamed officer in the War Department, quoted in ibid., 215.

13. Quoted in ibid., 230.

14. Anonymous, quoted in Gatewood, *Black Americans*, 282.

15. Roth, *Muddy Glory*, 65.

16. Gatewood, *Black Americans*, 280.

17. Quoted in David Lawrence Fritz, "The Philippine Question: American Civil/Military Policy in the Philippines, 1898–1905" (Ph.D. dissertation, University of Texas, 1977), 208.

18. "Report of Major-General Otis," May 14, 1900, in *The Annual Report of the War Department for the Fiscal Year Ended June 30, 1900*, vol. 1, part 4 (Washington, D.C.: Government Printing Office, 1900), 207.

19. Lawton to Brig. Gen. Theodore Schwan, October 25, 1899, in ibid., 221.

20. Lawton to Schwan, November 7, 1899, in ibid., 231; Lawton to Schwan, November 9, 1899, in ibid., 232.

21. Lawton to Schwan, November 12, 1899, in ibid., 234.

22. Report for 1900, quoted in James H. Blount, *The American Occupation of the Philippines, 1898–1912* (New York: Putnam, 1912), 242.

23. Quoted in ibid., 247.

24. John R.M. Taylor, *The Philippine Insurrection against the United States*, vol. 5 (Pasay City, Philippines: Eugenio Lopez Foundation, 1971), 5.

25. Ibid., 5:4–5.

26. Ibid., 5:5.

27. March to Young, December 7, 1899, in *The Annual Report of the War Department for the Fiscal Year Ended June 30, 1900*, vol. 1,

part 4 (Washington, D.C.: Government Printing Office, 1900), 319.

28. Taylor, *Philippine Insurrection,* 5:12.

5. One War Ends, Another Begins

1. Lawton to Brig. Gen. Theodore Schwan, December 9, 1899, in *The Annual Report of the War Department for the Fiscal Year Ended June 30, 1900,* vol. 1, part 4 (Washington, D.C.: Government Printing Office, 1899), 302.
2. McCalla to Young, December 14, 1899, in ibid., 336.
3. Col. A. H. Bowman, "Official Report of the 25th Regiment, 1899–1902" in John H. Nankivell, ed., *History of the Twenty-Fifth Regiment United States Infantry, 1869–1926* (New York: Negro University Press, 1927), 90.
4. Both quotes from William T. Schenck to the *Denver Daily News,* January 6, 1900, in Nankivell, ed., *History of the Twenty-Fifth Regiment,* 101–102.
5. Quoted in Frank Lewis Prue, 9th U.S.V. Infantry, "A Ninth Infantry Soldier's Experiences in the Philippine Insurrection," 23, Spanish-American War Survey, Military History Institute, Carlisle, Pa.
6. Allan Millett, *The General: Robert Bullard and Officership in the United States Army 1881–1925* (Westport, Conn.: Greenwood, 1975), 126–28.
7. Ibid., 130. See also Bullard's report on the matter in *The Annual Report of the War Department for the Fiscal Year Ended June 30, 1900,* 1:385.
8. Schwan to Otis, February 8, 1900, in *The Annual Report of the War Department for the Fiscal Year Ended June 30, 1900,* 1:390.
9. Quoted in John Gates, *Schoolboys and Krags: The United States Army in the Philippines, 1898–1902* (Westport, Conn.: Greenwood, 1973), 129.
10. Norman G. Owen, "Winding Down the War in Albay, 1900–1903," *Pacific Historical Review* 48 (1979): 557–89, 575–76.
11. David A. Lockmiller, *Enoch H. Crowder: Soldier, Lawyer, and Statesman* (Columbia: University of Missouri Studies, 1955), 76–77, has a discussion of the new legal code.

12. Quoted in ibid., 133.
13. Joseph P. McCallus, ed., *Gentleman Soldier: John Clifford Brown and the Philippine-American War* (College Station: Texas A&M University Press, 2004), 196.
14. LaWall, Company I, 27th Regiment, U.S. Volunteers, "Sixteen Months in the Philippines," Military History Institute, Carlisle, Pa.
15. Otis telegram to Adjutant-General, May 3, 1900, in Graham Cosmas, ed., *Correspondence Relating to the War with Spain, Including the Insurrection in the Philippine Islands and the China Relief Expedition* (Washington, D.C.: Center for Military History, 1993), 1164.
16. Quoted in Russell Roth, *Muddy Glory: America's "Indian Wars" in the Philippines* (W. Hanover, Mass.: Christopher Publishing House, 1981), 18.
17. Otis telegram to Adjutant-General, May 4, 1900, in Cosmas, ed., *Correspondence*, 1165.
18. Quoted in H. Wayne Morgan, *William McKinley and His America* (Kent, Ohio: Kent State University Press, 2003), 371.
19. Quoted in ibid., 374.
20. Roosevelt to Lodge, July 1, 1899, in Henry Cabot Lodge, ed., *Selections from the Correspondence of Theodore Roosevelt and Henry Cabot Lodge, 1884–1918* (New York: Scribner, 1925), 404.
21. Roosevelt to Lodge, December 11, 1899, in ibid., 426.
22. Roosevelt to Lodge, February 2, 1900, in ibid., 448.
23. Walter LaFeber, "Election of 1900," in Arthur M. Schlesinger, Jr., Fred L. Israel, and William P. Hansen, eds., *History of American Presidential Elections, 1789–2001*, vol. 5 (Philadelphia: Chelsea House, 2002), 1875–1962.
24. Ibid., 1886.
25. Roosevelt to Lodge, June 25, 1900, in Lodge, ed., *Selections*, 465.
26. Quoted in William Carl Spielman, *William McKinley: Stalwart Republican* (New York: Exposition Press, 1954), 172.
27. R. Ernest Dupuy and William Banner, *The Little Wars of the United States* (New York: Hawthorn Books, 1968), 84.
28. Edward Coffman, *The Hilt of the Sword: The Career of Peyton C. March* (Madison: University of Wisconsin Press, 1966), 18.
29. Stanley Karnow, *In Our Image: America's Empire in the Philippines* (New York: Random House, 1989), 171.

30. Rowland T. Berthoff, "Taft and MacArthur, 1900–1901: A Study in Civil-Military Relations," *World Politics* 5, no. 2 (January 1953): 196–213.

31. Kenneth Ray Young, *The General's General: The Life and Times of Arthur MacArthur* (Boulder, Colo.: Westview Press, 1994), 260–61.

32. LaWall, "Sixteen Months in the Philippines."

33. A. B. Feuer, ed., *America at War: The Philippines, 1898–1913* (Westport, Conn.: Praeger, 2002), 183–84.

34. Quoted in McCallus, *Gentleman Soldier*, 230.

35. LaWall, "Sixteen Months in the Philippines."

36. Quoted in Brian McAllister Linn, "Intelligence and Low-Intensity Conflict in the Philippine War, 1899–1902," in *Intelligence and National Security* 6, no. 1 (January 1991): 90–114.

37. Quoted in William B. Gatewood, Jr., *Black Americans and the White Man's Burden* (Urbana: University of Illinois Press, 1975), 269.

38. Lowell Thomas, *Woodfill of the Regulars: A True Story of Adventure from the Arctic to the Argonne* (New York: Doubleday, 1929), 45.

39. Gatewood, *Black Americans*, 199.

40. John R.M. Taylor, *The Philippine Insurrection against the United States: A Compilation of Documents with Notes and Introduction* (Pasay City, Philippines: Eugenio Lopez Foundation, 1971), 5:106.

41. Lt. Col. Julio Herrera to Local Presidentes, May 6, 1900, in ibid., 194.

42. Quoted in Berthoff, "Taft and MacArthur," 199.

43. LaWall, "Sixteen Months in the Philippines."

44. MacArthur to Adjutant-General, Washington, D.C., September 19, 1900, in Cosmas, ed., *Correspondence*, 1211.

45. Quoted in Young, *The General's General*, 282.

46. Quoted in Andrew Birtle, "The U.S. Army's Pacification of Marinduque, Philippine Islands, April 1900–April 1901," *Journal of Military History* 61, no. 2 (April 1997): 255–82, 266.

47. Berthoff, "Taft and MacArthur," 202.

48. Birtle, "U.S. Army's Pacification," 263.

49. Ibid., 1222.

50. William Henry Scott, *Ilocano Responses to American Aggression, 1900–1901* (Quezon City, Philippines: New Day Publishers, 1986), 162.

51. Quoted in Frank Friedel, "General Orders 100 and Military Government," *Mississippi Valley Historical Review* 32, no. 4 (March 1946): 541–56, 549.

52. John S. Reed, "External Discipline during Counterinsurgency: A Philippine War Case-Study, 1900–01," *Journal of American–East Asian Relations* 4, no. 1 (spring 1995): 29–48, 37, 35.

53. Howard K. Beale, *Theodore Roosevelt and the Rise of America to World Power* (Baltimore: Johns Hopkins University Press, 1956), 65.

54. Quoted in ibid., 71.

55. George Knox in the *Indianapolis Freeman*, quoted in Gatewood, *Black Americans*, 183.

56. Feuer, ed., *America at War*, 185.

57. Taylor, *Philippine Insurrection*, 373.

58. MacArthur telegram to Adjutant-General, December 3, 1900, in Cosmas, ed., *Correspondence*, 1232.

59. Scott, *Ilocano Responses*, 161.

60. Taylor, *Philippine Insurrection*, 134.

61. Ibid., 131.

62. Reed, "External Discipline," 49.

63. LaWall, "Sixteen Months in the Philippines."

64. Evan Wyatt, 8th U.S. Infantry, Army Service Experiences Questionnaire, Military History Institute, Carlisle, Pa.

65. Feuer, ed., *America at War*, 186.

66. Kobbé to Headquarters Department of Mindanao and Jolo, January 22, 1901, in *Annual Report of the War Department, 1901*, vol. 1, part 4 (Washington, D.C.: Government Printing Office, 1901), 273.

67. Quoted in Donald Smythe, *Guerilla Warrior: The Early Life of John J. Pershing* (New York: Scribner, 1973), 62.

68. Lt. H. S. Howland, quoted in Frank E. Vandiver, *Black Jack: The Life and Times of John J. Pershing*, vol. 1 (College Station: Texas A&M University Press, 1977), 257.

69. Birkhimer to the Adjutant-General, Department of Mindanao and Jolo, January 15, 1901, in *Annual Report of the War Department, 1901*, 1: 279.

70. Report of Maj. M. M. McNamee to Adjutant-General, Department of Mindanao and Jolo, December 29, 1900, in ibid., 291.

71. Birkhimer to the Adjutant-General, Department of Mindanao and Jolo, January 15, 1901, in ibid., 276.

6. "Satisfactory and Encouraging"

1. Graham Cosmas, ed., *Correspondence Relating to the War with Spain, Including the Insurrection in the Philippine Islands and the China Relief Expedition* (Washington, D.C.: Center for Military History, 1993), 1241.
2. A. B. Feuer, ed., *America at War: The Philippines, 1898–1913* (Westport, Conn.: Praeger, 2002), 191.
3. W. H. Scott, *Ilocano Responses to American Aggression, 1900–1901* (Quezon City, Philippines: New Day Publishers, 1986), 161–78.
4. Much of this account is drawn from Funston's report to MacArthur. See "Frederick Funston Report on Capture of Aguinaldo," in H. P. Legg, 1898-W-799, Company F, 17th U.S. Infantry, Military History Institute, Carlisle, Pa.
5. Emilio Aguinaldo and Vicente Albano Pacis, *A Second Look at America* (New York: Robert Speller & Sons, 1957), 16.
6. Herbert M. Reddy, U.S. Infantry, 6th Regiment, "Ridin' Herd in the Philippines," Spanish-American War Survey, Military History Institute, Carlisle, Pa. Reddy caught a glimpse of Aguinaldo watching the game.
7. John R.M. Taylor, *The Philippine Insurrection Against the United States* (Pasay City, Philippines: Eugenio Lopez Foundation, 1971), 5: 378.
8. Aguinaldo and Pacis, *A Second Look at America*, 129.
9. Ibid.
10. Reddy, "Ridin' Herd in the Philippines."
11. Ibid.
12. Ibid.
13. Ibid.
14. William B. Gatewood, Jr., *Black Americans and the White Man's Burden* (Urbana: University of Illinois Press, 1975), 277.
15. Scot Ngozi-Brown, "African American Soldiers and Filipinos: Racial Imperialism, Jim Crow, and Social Relations," *Journal of Negro History* 82, 1 (winter 1997): 42–53. Blakeny letter quoted in William Gatewood, Jr., *"Smoked Yankees" and the Struggle for Empire: Letters from Negro Soldiers, 1898–1902* (Fayetteville: University of Arkansas Press, 1987), 311.
16. Edmund Morris, *Theodore Rex* (New York: Modern Library, 2001), 30.
17. Ibid., 3.

18. Ibid., 13–15.
19. James Taylor, ed., *The Massacre of Balangiga: Being an Authentic Account by Several of the Few Survivors* (Joplin, Mo.: McCarn Printing, 1931), 23.
20. Ibid., 7, 11.
21. Ibid., 38.
22. Ibid., 1.
23. David L. Fritz, "Before the 'Howling Wilderness': The Military Career of Jacob Hurd Smith, 1862–1902," *Military Affairs* 43, no. 4 (December 1979): 186–90.
24. Brian Linn, *The Philippine War, 1899–1902* (Lawrence: University Press of Kansas, 2000), 312, for example.
25. William Thomas Keane, 8th Regiment U.S.V., Army Service Experiences Questionnaire, Military History Institute, Carlisle, Pa.
26. For the surrender of Lukhban, see Eugene F. Ganley, "Mountain Chase," *Military Affairs* 24, no. 4 (winter 1960–61): 203–10.
27. Glenn Anthony May, "150,000 Missing Filipinos: A Demographic Crisis in Batangas, 1887–1903," *Annales de Démographie Historique* 21 (1985): 215–43, 237.
28. Forrest Pogue, *George C. Marshall: Education of a General, 1880–1939* (New York: Viking, 1963), 75.
29. Ibid.
30. Ibid.
31. Ibid.
32. Quoted in Morris, *Theodore Rex*, 101.
33. Quoted in ibid., 104.
34. Pvt. Evan E. Wyatt, 1898–236, 8th U.S. Infantry, Military History Institute, Carlisle, Pa.

Conclusion: A Most Favored Race

1. Quoted in Brian McAllister Linn, "The Long Twilight of the Frontier Army," *Western Historical Quarterly* 27, no. 2 (summer 1996): 141–67, 158.
2. Raymond Ileto, "The Philippine-American War: Friendship and Forgetting," in *Vestiges of War: The Philippine-American War and the Aftermath of an Imperial Dream, 1899–1999* (New York: New York University Press, 2002), 3.
3. David Joel Steinberg, "An Ambiguous Legacy: Years at War in the

Philippines," *Public Affairs* 45, no. 2 (summer 1972): 168–90, 179.

4. Emilio Aguinaldo and Vicente Albano Pacis, *A Second Look at America* (New York: Robert Speller & Sons, 1957), 16.

5. This argument is, of course, not original with me. See Benedict Anderson, *Imagined Communities* (London: Verso, 1991), as well as Benedict Anderson, *The Spectre of Comparisons: Nationalism, Southeast Asia, and the World* (London: Verso, 1998), 193–264.

6. Quoted in Linn, "Long Twilight," 151.

Acknowledgments

This book would not have been possible without the help of a large number of people. Thomas LeBien was kind enough to take a flier on an unknown scholar. Eric Rauchway got the project rolling and had solid words of advice along the way. The staff of the Van Pelt Library at the University of Pennsylvania were generous with their time and effort, although they signally failed to pry open a set of broken compact shelves. The archivists at the Military History Institute in Carlisle, Pennsylvania, were, as always, remarkably thoughtful and efficient. At Alvernia College, my colleagues—Victoria Williams, Jerry Vigna, Tim Blessing, Donna Yarri, and Kevin Godfrey—have been constantly helpful. President Lawrence Mazzeno and Provost Charles Perkins, obligingly enough, hired and then tenured me. Joel

Silbey was both a useful sounding board and a supportive father. Rosemary Silbey occupied a similar role on the maternal side. Madeline Silbey raced me to the finish line, and won by being born weeks ahead of the final sentence of the manuscript. None of this would be possible without Mari. To say that she was supportive simply mocks the inadequacy of the English language. This book is for her.

Index

INDEX

Printed in the USA
CPSIA information can be obtained
at www.ICGtesting.com
LVHW091138150724
785511LV00005B/406

9 780809 096619